Improvement
and Enlightenment

Improvement
and Enlightenment

Proceedings of the
Scottish Historical Studies Seminar
University of Strathclyde
1987–88

Edited by

T. M. DEVINE

JOHN DONALD PUBLISHERS LTD
EDINBURGH

ISBN 0 85976 258 0   .

The publishers acknowledge the
financial assistance of the Scottish
Arts Council in the publication
of this volume.

Phtotypeset by Print Origination (NW) Ltd., Formby
Printed in Great Britain by Bell & Bain Ltd., Glasgow

Preface

This volume presents the proceedings of the Scottish Historical Studies seminar held at the University of Strathclyde during the academic session 1987-88. The seminar was established to provide a focus for advanced scholarship in the developing field of Scottish social history. Each year a different theme or period is selected for special attention and leading scholars present their most recent research results on key issues. Where possible, the approach of the seminar is interdisciplinary and attracts an audience of sociologists, historical geographers and literary scholars in addition to historians.

The papers in this volume focus on one of the most formative and vital phases in Scottish historical development, a period when the structure of society began to alter with the onset of industrialisation and urbanisation, the establishment of new political and cultural relationships with England and the vigour of eighteenth-century intellectual activity. All the essays are original studies which explore a variety of aspects of this crucial period from a range of disciplinary perspectives.

T. M. Devine

Contributors

T.M. Devine
Professor in Scottish History, University of Strathclyde

R.A. Houston
Lecturer in Modern History, University of St. Andrews

Thomas A. Markus
Emeritus Professor of Architecture and Building Science, University of Strathclyde

Rosalind Mitchison
Professor Emeritus of Social History, University of Edinburgh

Andrew Noble
Senior Lecturer in English Studies, University of Strathclyde

T.C. Smout
Professor of Scottish History, University of St. Andrews

Contents

1

Problems of Nationalism, Identity and Improvement in later Eighteenth-Century Scotland

T. C. Smout

Why did full-blown nationalism not emerge in Scotland around the start of the nineteenth century? Scotland was an ancient nation-state, forged in the fourteenth-century wars of independence, compromised by the Union of Crowns in 1603 and the Union of Parliaments in 1707, but involved in eighteenth-century rebellions in which Jacobite claimants promised to repeal at least the latter union. It had its own distinctive institutions of civil society, the Prebyterian Church of Scotland as by law established, its five universities, its corpus of civil law with its own professional closed shops, its famed parish schools: all enclaves for the careers of the middling ranks from which Englishmen were effectively excluded. Compared to many a European 'historyless nation'(Engel's phrase) whose intellectuals constructed an effective nationalism from much less promising materials, Scotland looked to have a flying start. Why, then, did the horse refuse to leave the starting gate with the Americans in 1775 or the Irish in 1782, or the French in 1793, or in 1815, or 1832, or 1848? Why did it only lift its head with the cranky Scottish Rights movement of the 1850s and lukewarm Home Rule movement of the 1880s, and only begin to show much animation after the First World War? In the heady days of the 1970s, when the SNP looked set for a sudden gallop through the British political field with potentially momentous effects, political scientists puzzled over the problem of its earlier retardation, sometimes and most interestingly, as part of a general investigation into the origins and nature of nationalism.

Tom Nairn's investigation and explanation, in *The Break-up of Britain*, has been one of the most influential.[1] It follows a neo-Marxist thesis originating from Ernest Gellner that as the economic and political revolutions beginning in eighteenth-century Britain and France spread outwards, the European middle class, excited but unprepared, were forced into a nationalist reaction. 'A tidal wave of modernization', as Nairn expresses it, swept down on the Continent, compelling other nations to 'demand progress not as it is thrust upon them initially by the metropolitan centre but "on their own terms.".' And what were these terms? They involved the bourgeois intelligentsia of different countries using nationalist rhetoric both to mobilise a self-conscious 'people' to destroy the absolutism (sometimes native, sometimes alien) of the *ancien régime*, and then to construct around themselves and the 'people' a fence of nationalist consciousness to keep out the political and economic imperialism of, in the first instance, the French and the British. The Scots, however, did not need this strategy because they were already part of the aggressive centre, not of the defensive periphery. The Scottish bourgeois were already secure; they were not affected by the 'tidal wave of modernization' that swept over Europe because they were riding on its aggressive crest. Only when most of the benefits of political and economic empire began to be withdrawn from the Scottish middle class in the first half of the twentieth century did the latent nationalism of an ancient quasi-nation start to operate. In other words, until recently the union paid the Scots too well for them to worry about nationalism, but when it stopped paying well nationalism was ready to hand.

Nairn's analysis met criticism from Anthony Smith in two respects.[2] First, Smith argued that only if the British and French states were already themselves nationalist would the population of other lands respond in a nationalist manner, thrusting back imperialist ethnic pretensions by defensive ethnic pretensions of their own. That, he says, 'assumes the independence, and historical priority, of ethnic nationalism from the uneven development of capitalism'. He supports this by reference to the English nationalism of Bolingbroke and Burke, and to the French nationalism of Siéyès. He further doubts if the timing in Europe fits Nairn's model: Greek, Serb, Polish, Corsican and Swiss nationalism, for example, clearly antedate any 'tidal wave' of capitalism in their respective territories. The American example is more telling still.

Next, Smith makes an obvious yet invaluable point about dual allegiancies.[3] Modern Scotland, he suggests, is typical of a set of countries whose citizens possess what he calls 'concentric loyalties'—to their own ethnic communities, and to the states in which they have been incorporated so long. Most twentieth-century Bretons, Catalans, Scots and Welshmen also see themselves as Frenchmen, Spaniards and Britons in addition to their ethnic-national identities. One loyalty in no way necessarily excludes the other. But the present 'ethnic revival' of which modern Scottish nationalism is a striking example is itself 'a chronological continuum of older nationalism', i.e. these concentric loyalties are themselves of ancient lineage. Smith's idea of concentric loyalties having existed for at least 200 years is at least as useful as Nairn's image of a latent nationalism, suddenly emerging to fulfill a historic role when the spoils of Empire are finished. It helps to explain the strange variations in intensity of Scottish nationalist feeling, rampant in the 1970s, in decline for most of the 1980s when British nationalism staged a recovery despite an economic situation that might lead one to expect Nairn's 'break-up of Britain'.

The debate nevertheless leaves a historian with uneasy feelings, partly because neither Nairn nor Smith (their concerns legitimately being elsewhere) investigates the language that eighteenth- and early nineteenth-century people actually used about their own identity. We might begin by heeding Jonathan Clark's warning to his fellow historians of Hanoverian England to see the period in its own terms and not to attempt to describe a proto-motor-car from the dimensions of a sedan chair.[4] We should not expect to encounter anywhere in the eighteenth-century world the full-blown nineteenth-century nationalism of the political scientist, what Gerald Newman at one point calls an 'all-consuming, civic and egalitarian sentiment' and at another an 'all-consuming sentiment attached to the symbols of the people and the collective personality, and inclined towards radical innovation'. On the other hand, we are already beyond his 'mere patriotism', defined as a 'primitive feeling of loyalty', confined largely to the aristocracy, focusing on military matters and the person of the king, and conservative in tone.[5] What we do get are complex feelings of national identity that need to be examined on their own terms.

Nowhere in Europe was this sense of national identity more complex than in Scotland. Janet Adam Smith, for example, in a pioneering article examined Hume, Alexander Carlyle, the Adam brothers, Boswell, Allan Ramsay the elder, Robert Fergusson and Burns;[6] she found in the first three a strong sense of loyalty both to Scotland and to Britain, in Boswell bursts of an idiosyncratic Scottish anti-Union feeling which nevertheless went with political loyalty to Britain, in the poets a stronger sense of the value of Scottishness, a weaker sense of the virtues of Britain, but in none of them consistent and practical opposition either to the union or to England. By previous definitions their emotions were less than nationalist but more than merely patriotic and all clearly expressed strongly held feelings of national identity.

Digging deeper, it is actually possible to discover in eighteenth-century Scottish writing a few fairly fierce statements about England and the English which would seem to qualify as nationalist, if one of nationalism's marks is an obsessive sense of being oppressed by a neighbour nation. The most famous of these are in Thomas Muir's 'Memorials on Scotland' written from France in 1797-8 when the author was seeking political and financial support from the Directorate: they describe the Union as a fraud (but Burns and Boswell would not have disagreed with that), the rule of Westminster as English oppression and the Scots as thirsting for liberty and an independent Republic.[7] John Brims, in an important paper,[8] has recently drawn attention to the pamphlet of a former clerk of the Sasine Office, James Thomson Callender, published in 1792, which described the machinations of 'our southern masters, to extirpate as fast as possible every manufacture in this country that interferes with their own', and which similarly interpreted Scottish eighteenth-century history in terms of conquest and subjection by a hostile nation. The following year Lord Daer wrote to Charles Grey warning him of a widespread radical nationalist sentiment which summed up the eighteenth-century constitutional relationship as 'Scotland has long groaned under the chains of England' and because 'We have been the worse of every connection hitherto with you, the Friends of Liberty in Scotland have almost universally been enemies to the Union with England'. In the Militia disturbances of 1797 there were rumours in Perthshire about demands to reduce rents and ministers' stipends and 'making the King reside at Edinburgh'.[9] There is enough here to indicate an alternative view of the Union to that of 'the fount from which all blessings flow' which was so common in 'concentric loyalty' Scots. Nevertheless, Brims concludes his examination of the problem with the undoubtedly correct conclusion that 'the constitutional relationship between Scotland and England was for most, if certainly not all, Scottish "Jacobins" a matter of small importance.'

If downright anti-English, anti-Union, clearly separatist sentiments are hard to find, the opposite pole of completely integrationist sentiments where Scots show no consciousness of or will to be in any sense different from the English are much more unusual. The Earl of Cromarty at the time of the Union had expressed the hope that the old names of Scotland and England would completely disappear, but he did not believe that former loyalties would be swallowed up in a new Britain. Similarly, his political ally Sir John Clerk of Penicuik combined a vast pride in having been an architect of Union with a lifetime's dedication to the archaeology of Roman Scotland, which he interpreted as the relics of ancient virtuous, national struggles against absorption.[10] Later in the century Scottish MPs and country gentlemen, both in public language and private conversation, sometimes referred to Britain as 'England', adopting in this respect the common habit of the

English themselves. Yet there was hardly a single articulate figure in eighteenth-century Scotland who did not at one time or another firmly and generally approvingly describe himself as a Scot. Is Adam Smith an exception? If so, it may be because of his own secretive nature which was so reluctant to reveal anything private about himself, rather than a personal obliteration of his consciousness of being Scottish. His opposition to that dearest and most patriotic cause of the Scottish *literati*, a national militia, was well known, yet apparently it rested on general principle which would omit the specific case of Scotland. John Robertson draws attention to a letter in which Smith expresses alarm lest the publication of Hooke's *Memoirs* of the Jacobite plots of 1707-8 might 'throw a damp upon *our* militia'.[11]

It is, then, undoubtedly correct to conclude that most Scots felt themselves to be both Scottish and British. And if Adam Smith is after all to be included among such people at one pole, the so-called 'nationalist poets', Robert Fergusson and Robert Burns, can readily be admitted at the other. Fergusson often speaks slightingly of England, but equally often, warmly of Britain: 'Thrice happy Britons . . . these are the sons that hem Britannia round from sudden innovation', 'cherished vigour in Britannia's sons', and so on.[12] Some of Burns's most patriotic and strongly-felt political poems refer to Britain. Take the *Twa dogs*, where the laird's hound laments the behaviour of his master's class as being not 'for Britain's guid', as the deluded sheepdog was simple enough to think, 'but for her destruction, wi' dissipation, feud an' faction'. Or take the *Ode for general Washington's birthday*, with its reference to 'the freeborn Briton's soul of fire', followed by stanzas referring separately to the historic *geist* of England and Scotland, and the *Birthday address to George III*, which deals with the tribulations of 'auld Britain' and 'British boys' without a word on Scotia's ills or Caledonia's neglected sons. Some find *The Dumfries volunteers*, 'Does haughty Gaul invasion threat', of 1795 an offensive retreat from the radical Paineite poems of the earlier 1790s, but in some ways its patriotic tone echoes the *Twa dogs* of 1786. In the former the irresponsible, cosmopolitan, Frenchified laird neglects his civic duties and 'in a frolic daft to Hague or Calais takes a waft, To make a tour an' tak a whirl, To learn bon ton an' see the worl': and the health of Britain suffers. In the latter French pretensions to interfere in British affairs are rejected: 'never but by British hands, maun British wrangs he righted'; it did not say there were no British wrongs, but 'while we sing God save the king, we'll ne'er forget the people'.

What Scots did not feel themselves to be was English. If Scotland was a province, or a nation (and Scots could use both terms), England was another province, or a nation. And to England they had united in 1707 on equal terms, as a partner. Scots often had no objection to admitting that Scotland was a junior partner, led by a more opulent and, perhaps, more mature sister kingdom, as Alexander Wedderburn put it in an oft-quoted passage in the *Edinburgh Review* in 1756:

> If countries have their ages with respect to improvement North Britain may be considered as in a state of early youth, guided and supported by the mature strength of her kindred country.[13]

What Scots did object to was English assumptions that they, the southerners, were the only true Britons, the only kingdom in the United Kingdom, the majority with the right to overrule the traditions and institutions of the minority at their whim. Hence the tin-drum fury with which the *literati* pressed their claims to a militia against the doubts of the Westminster establishment that assumed most Scots even in the 1760s to be at least crypto-Jacobite.[14] Hence the depth of feeling with which lawyers and others defended the pre-Reformation law of marriage from Hardwicke's Act,[15] or the full complement of fifteen judges on the Court of Session against ministerial attempts to reduce it to ten.[16] In the latter case they pretended in 1785, forcefully but bogusly, that the Act of Union could not be amended except by the consent 'of the people of Scotland', whatever that phrase might mean. Hence the reaction of the town councils of the main burghs to the Mortmain Bill of 1773 which threatened to draw Scottish charitable endowments into government funds at 3%. Robert Fergusson in his most nationalist vein in *Ghaists* made George Heriot proclaim:

> Black be the day that e'er to England's ground
> Scotland was eikit by the Union's bond,

imagining the objects of his charity 'doomed to keep a lasting Lent/ Starving for England's weel at three per cent'.

Hence, too, the visceral feelings of indignation with which Scottish visitors to London repelled English prejudice. As Hume put it to Gilbert Elliot of Minto in 1764:

> Some hate me because I am not a Whig, some because I am not a Christian, and all because I am a Scotsman. Can you seriously talk of my continuing an Englishman? Am I, or are you, an Englishman? Will they allow us to be so?[17]

Yet he was the same man who could speak unselfconsciously of 'London being the capital of my own country', and who submitted his prose to Wilkes (of all people) to iron out the barbarous Scotticisms that might betray a provincial origin. Anxiety about a Scottish accent, or writing in Scottish idioms, was widespread among the *literati* and among their allies in the landed classes, the latter, when they could afford it, sending their children to school or university in England to learn polite manners and speech, in order to assist their career chances on a southern, wider, stage. Obviously such people became much more 'Anglicised' than the stay-at-home lower orders.

But what psychic energies emerged from pronouncing oneself to be a Scotsman? In Hume's case, perhaps, the one basic to most of us who proclaim our roots in any locality or nation, a feeling that we need not apologise too much for being who or what we are, a sense of being at least as good as the next man even if we talk funny and eat our peas with a knife. Among the Wordsworthian Romantic poets, who have been identified as an important force in the forging of nineteenth-century nationalism out of such gut feelings, a sense of one's true worth as a human being was intertwined with awareness of one's roots in a locality. This twist is already there in Burns. In the *Vision* of 1786 the name of the muse who proclaimed the poet 'my *own* inspired Bard' was not Britannia or even Scotia but Coila. He was a Kyle nationalist, the innermost and most intense of the three concentric loyalties that made him, if you like, also a Scottish nationalist and a British nationalist. And this intense sense of place was a sense of sincerity as opposed to artificiality, of a sense of being 'oneself' as opposed to pretending to be something else—foreign, exotic, unnative, insincere. Robert Burns admired Henry Mackenzie, a writer who to modern taste seems almost totally insipid: but the point of *The Man of Feeling* was that he elevated sincerity above fashion and deprecated what was foreign compared to what was homespun. The tirade in the *Twa dogs* against a lord on the Grand Tour who 'at Vienna or Versailles, rives his father's auld entails' and 'down Italian Vista startles, Whore hunting amang groves o' myrtles' can be effectively paralleled in *The Man of Feeling*'s complaint: 'From this bear-garden of the pedagogue, a raw unprincipled boy is turned loose upon the world to travel, without any ideas but those of improving his dress at Paris, or starting into taste by gazing on some paintings at Rome'.[18] The metropolitan, the cosmopolitan, is the vicious: the local, the native, is the true. And this is the case even though Mackenzie, wishing to be accepted as a British author and having neither the vision nor the moral courage of Burns, consistently refers to *The Man of Feeling* himself as an Englishman.

One of the problems that the Scots always had with their concentric loyalties is that they were not, and are not, shared by Englishmen. A

Scot, James Thomson, wrote *Rule Britannia*: Britannia bore on her shield the Union Jack with the Saltire and St George's cross; to Scots this represented a union of equal kingdoms. But to Englishmen, Britannia was solely an English lass. To England, Scotland was akin to Ireland, a conquered province of questionable loyalty; England was Britain, Britain was England: it would have seemed as absurd for the average eighteenth-century Englishman to distinguish an inner loyalty to a smaller England from an outer loyalty to a greater Britain as it was natural for a Scot to make his analogous distinction.

It was the discovery of this, by Scottish visitors to the xenophobic London of the 1740s, 1750s and 1760s, which strained their loyalty to breaking point. It was when Boswell witnessed the mobbing of two Scottish officers in Highland dress at Covent Garden in 1762 to cries of 'No Scots! No Scots! Out with them!' that he jumped on the benches to roar: 'Damn you, you rascals':

> I hated the English; I wished from my soul that the Union was broke and that we might give them another battle of Bannockburn.[19]

Here we have a very clear instance of a Scottish intellectual encountering what Isaiah Berlin in his classic examination of nationalism calls 'a patronising or disparaging attitude towards the traditional values of a society' which leads to 'wounded pride and a sense of humiliation in its most socially conscious members', and which also in due course 'produces anger and self-assertion'—in effect, it should produce full-blown nationalism out of mere patriotic consciousness.[20] But it did not work like that on Boswell or his friends. Like so many of his class and time, he was a bundle of jumbled identities, at one moment a sentimental Jacobite ('all agreed in our love of the Royal Family of Stuart'), at another an affectionate Hanoverian ('I love from my soul "Great George Our King" '), at one moment refusing to visit Wilkes in gaol because 'I am a Scotch laird and a Scotch lawyer and a Scotch married man . It would not be decent', at another celebrating what he describes as his own 'English juiciness of mind'. In fact, he found Edinburgh constraining, London liberating, the Scottish literary stage narrow, the English one broad. In the end, like so many Scots similarly placed, he swallowed his pride and put up with insult and disparagement in the cause of pursuing more than a provincial career.[21]

There were many Scots who reacted like Boswell. Surely Tom Nairn got it right here. For the intelligentsia and for the bourgeoisie, the Union provided material opportunity which as a class they were not prepared to pass up for a few insults. The parts played by the great political managers, Islay and especially Dundas, were vital to ensure the steady flow of patronage to reward Scots with political spoil, great and small— offices within British civil government service, naval and army commissions at home and abroad, plums from the East India Company pie. It is not irrelevant to consider that loyal Scotland obtained what rebellious America lacked in the eighteenth century, a career structure for her sons in British service. If the Union had not been made to work in this way, if English statesmen had been as crudely anti-Scottish as the English mob, would Scotland have stayed so supportive of the concept of Great Britain? There is no reason to think so at all.

It is interesting to consider in this context Gerald Newman's new book, *The Rise of English Nationalism, 1740-1830*. In many ways it is annoying. His claims singlehandedly to have discovered English nationalism do scant justice to the work of Anthony Smith, among others, who had already firmly placed it in the pre-industrial revolution period. Nor does his belief that English xenophobia was new in the mid-eighteenth century square with what English historians know about anti-French and anti-Dutch feeling in the later seventeenth century. Above all to a Scottish historian, Newman is unaware that there is any distinction between a Scotsman and an Englishman; for instance, he quotes, in a chapter called 'The Moral Elevation of the English National Identity', James Watt's observations on his greatest invention: 'If I merit it some of my countrymen, inspired by the *Amor Patriae* may say: *Hoc a Scoto factum fuit*'.[22] Any such hint of Scottish patriotism is for Newman a reinforcement of the reality of an emergent English nationalism, rather than the assertion of an expatriate against English assumptions of superiority. His blindness extends to not even noticing in some of the contemporary illustrations to his own book that one of the depicted enemies of the true-born Englishman, in alliance with the false and apish French, is the needy and mendicant Scot. Herbert Atherton's splendid study of English political cartoons shows how prevalent, especially at the time of the Jacobite rising and the Bute ministry, was hatred of the Scots, taking a bitter, racist tone, portraying them as poverty-stricken, grasping, servile, treacherous, out for English jobs and gold and maltreating Britannia shamefully.[23] It would be unthinkable for any illustrator in Scotland to have turned the tables and portrayed the English as greedy, arrogant, domineering, insolent and corrupt, though with at least as much justice it could have been done.

However, this astigmatism in Newman's vision does not altogether detract from his central proposition, which is that beginning approximately at the time of Hogarth, British (or English) intellectuals launched an attack on the cosmopolitan, polite, foreign, and especially

French and Italian manners of the elite as being artificial, unhealthy and corrupt, and built up in distinction a model of the homely, sincere, true Briton, i.e. beef-eating Englishman, the frank and manly John Bull: in due course this became a way of, in some sense, mobilising 'the people', full of native Saxon virtue, against 'the aristocracy', corrupted by French guile and insincerity. As the idea developed it gave strength to the cause first of the elder Pitt, then to Wilkes, then to Cartwright and to the County Freeholders and other anti-parliamentarian reformers of the 1780s. It ended up being the dominant image that the English had of themselves in the nineteenth century, an image to which the nobility and other political leaders themselves had to conform to survive. The complacent Victorian Englishman with his innate moral superiority to every other race and nation ultimately reigned supreme.

When we see how Scottish intellectuals fitted themselves into this scheme, it is easy to understand how Newman assumed that Scots were only a subspecies of Englishmen. Even Fergusson is capable of writing poems like *Good eating* and *Fashion* in praise of roast beef, equating luxury, effeminacy and decay with France and Italy, and exclaiming 'Britons beware of Fashion's luring wiles'. Most interesting of all is Tobias Smollett, a man whom we know to have been very much upset by the anti-Scotch feeling that rocked London in the wake of the '45, at that time privately describing John Bull as vacillating between being 'abject and cowardly' before the Highlanders were defeated and 'haughty and valiant' afterwards.[24] Yet he made his literary reputation in the next two decades portraying the bluff, beef-eating, frank, true-born Englishman set against the French and the Frenchified men of fashion who set out to undermine the virtuous national spirit. It reached its most elaborate manifestation in *Humphrey Clinker* (1771) where effeminate French or Gallicised fashionable villains ('the fellow wears a solitaire, uses paint, and takes rappee with all the grimace of a French marquis') are set against three sincere heroes, Humphrey Clinker himself, an Englishman, Lismahago, a Scot, and Bramble, a Welshman. It ends in a marriage to three nice girls saved from seduction. As Newman sums it up:

> Smollett's last work was thus a benedictory farewell to all his British countrymen. In it he not only pounded away, as before, at the Quality and at Fashion, but hailed that extended world of the *Volk* which in following decades writers like Day and Cowper, Burns and Blake and Wordsworth, were to treat more appreciatively even than he.[25]

Certainly there is a link of sentiment between *Humphrey Clinker* and Burns' poems like the *Twa dogs* and the *Birthday address to George III*.

And in being anti-Quality and Fashion, there is a link between those poems of 1786 and the Paineite 'man's a man for a' that', with its scarifying—'gie fools their silks, and knaves their wine . . . their tinsel show, and a' that' of the early 1790s.

When we come to the mainstream of radical ideas we see very clearly again how concentric loyalty worked. It is interesting in this case that it did so among people who had nothing at all to hope for, career-wise, in an extended Britain. In 1776 John Cartwright had elaborated, as no writer before had ever done, the theory of the Norman Yoke, by which the primaeval English liberties of Saxon times had been lost by the Norman Conquest, yet waited to be reclaimed by the resolute action of modern Englishmen.[26] This led to a reading of English history as a whole series of events in which true-born Englishmen had asserted themselves against royal and aristocratic tyranny, from Hereward the Wake's rebellion against William the Bastard to Hampden's protest against Charles I, and beyond. All this was very appealing to the Scottish Friends of the People in the 1790s and their successors in the nineteenth century, and they adopted English history as their own by the simple device of arguing that in 1707 the new Britain inherited all the English and all the Scottish past, so the Scots plugged in to English history. Muir apparently argued at the first convention of the Friends of the People that the free constitution of Scotland was equally ancient to that of England, so by implication that Scotland's claims to liberty did not rest solely, perhaps not at all, on ancient English right or on the union.[27] We have seen that from exile in France he was explicitly and roundly to denounce the Union itself. But at his trial he defended himself solely by reference to the British Constitution, by which he meant the English one, with references to Locke, Sir Thomas More, to Hampden, Sidney and Marvell:

> Gentlemen, I am happy to find the people of Scotland rapidly advancing to a true sense of their Constitutional Liberties—to see them *demanding* to have the Constitution restored to its genuine principles, in order that they may behold their liberties confirmed, and their happiness established. That they should advance with more ardour in this cause, it was necessary that they should *know* the Constitution, what it had been in its vigour, and what it now is in its decay, by the corruption of men and of ages. And pray what did I do to effectuate these legal and enviable objects? . . . . the only book which I recommended to them was Henry's History of England, the best calculated, by its accuracy and plainness, to give them insight into the nature and progress of the Constitution.[28]

The plug-in theory of Scottish history could not be plainer stated.

On the other hand the appeal of the historicist approach to liberty in Scotland was obviously going to be even stronger if Scots themselves could find precedence in their own history for resistance to tyranny. The *Edinburgh Gazetteer* spotted the problem when in 1793 it wrote: 'The ancient Constitution of Scotland is covered with a thicker veil which the industry of the antiquary has not been able to penetrate, and therefore cannot be described with such accuracy as that of the Anglo Saxons; but if we may credit history or Tradition, our Celtic ancestors enjoyed a degree of political liberty not inferior to their more southern neighbours, until the introduction of the feudal system deprived them of the Primary rights'.[29] They were trying to whistle up a Celtic Democracy myth.

More readily to hand as mythic material were the Wars of Independence, with the poems of Barbour and Blind Harry still deep in popular consciousness. The example of Bruce and Wallace had been part even of the Jacobite armory of ideological resistance. Burns' heart had throbbed with patriotic zeal on the field of Bannockburn as early as 1787, six years before he composed his famous ode 'Scots! wha hae wi' Wallace bled' which was in the succeeding years to become so much a signature tune for radicals that in 1819 the magistrates of Paisley briefly imprisoned the town band for tapping out its tune. If Wallace could be recruited, who else? It was not easy to argue that the Jacobites stood for human rights, though Burns tried it on in 'Here's a health to them that's awa', with its lines 'May Liberty meet wi' success' and 'There's nane ever fear'd that the Truth should be heard/But they whom the Truth wad indite'. It was hard, however, to separate the Stewarts from the notion of tyranny, and radicals opted in the end to make heroes from the Covenanters' resistance to Charles II. At least from the early years of the nineteenth century it was commonplace to equate the struggle of the seventeenth-century humble folk for religious freedom (as this was portrayed) with the struggle of modern humble folk for civil rights.[30] This was strong even in Keir Hardie's generation, and among the Red Clydesiders. In the immediate circumstances of the early nineteenth century the authorities understood the import of all this very well, and expressed alarm at mass commemorative visits to the fields of both Bannockburn and Bothwell Brig.[31]

Yet because Scottish patriotism was concentric with British patriotism at all levels of society, the plug-in theory of history continued to prevail, and demands for universal suffrage were not accompanied by any rise of anti-English nationalism. The radicals were summoned onto the streets of Glasgow in 1820 with references to Magna Carta, and 'Scots! wha hae' was sung even in the Lancashire cotton factories in the 1830s as a rallying song for liberty.

Patriotic language, moreover, was not in Scotland by any means the monopoly of radicals: if it had been, they might have been able to make stronger use of its rhetoric. Part of the problem was that others were also accustomed to stamp national emotion on preoccupations quite different from those of Burns or Muir. Both John Robertson in his book on the Scottish militia problem, and John Dwyer in his book on *Virtuous Discourse*, have discussed the tradition of civic humanism blended with stoicism in late eighteenth-century Scotland, and shown how the *literati*, associated with the Moderate wing of the kirk, with the law and with the polite clubs and journals, used such tones, resting their patriotism simultaneously on a highly selective use of the intellectual Republicanism of Andrew Fletcher of Saltoun and on a wholehearted practical acceptance of the Union of 1707 and the Revolution of 1688 as the foundation of modern Britain. Fletcher's theories were really emasculated, as, taking their vocabulary but not their substance, the polite Whigs totally disregarded all the crucial things he had to say about alternative political structures as the path to true civic virtue.[32]

The cause to which the conformist intellectuals bent this language, though, had not much to do with chauvinism or xenophobia, or basic political criticism of the government, or the establishment of civil rights by the common people, but with the moral decay of the nation. Dwyer is particularly interested in the blending of the ancient discursive traditions, civic humanism with its 'stress upon the luxurious empire and concomitant corruption of moral autonomy', and stoicism, which 'accentuated the role of reason and self-command in the maintenance of the ethical personality', with the modern one of sensibility, which, drawing on Adam Smith's *Theory of Moral Sentiments*, could be seen as 'a characteristic that could be cultivated in order to neutralize the threat of luxury within the vulnerable modern state'.[33]

There is a curious, hollow, abstract quality in a lot of this debate, as if the 'state' for these intellectuals existed only as model, not as a real place. It was not, in Benedict Anderson's phrase, a coherently 'imagined community' from which modern nations are fashioned.[34] There were two reasons for this. Firstly in these polite circles the actual history of Scotland was declared barbarian, William Robertson having denigrated everything before 1688 as feudal darkness and anarchy in his famous *History*. In other words, there was no ancient virtue. A country whose intellectuals believe their history is rubbish is surely at a disadvantage when it comes to producing convincing nationalist energy.[35] It made itself a 'historyless nation'. Scott created new romantic images without really disturbing Robertson's essential story: M'Crie and others from the Covenanting tradition tried early in the nineteenth century to rehabilitate Knox and Melville, but it was an uphill task to unpick Robertson.

Secondly, the Gaelic-speaking Highlands were half of Scotland, and the most distinctive half, but were the eighteenth-century intellectuals to be proud of them or embarrassed about them? Were they quintessentially Scottish and virtuous or quintessentially barbarous, disloyal and to be forgotten about? The *literati* swithered, generally writing their presentations of history and society as though the Highlands did not exist, but in the Ossianic craze suddenly getting caught up in a mad fit of pride that Gaeldom after all embodied antique and heroic virtue on the grand scale. A group of tenants on Sir John Sinclair's estate in the 1790s nicely, if unwittingly, exposed the dilemma when they petitioned him for a Gaelic-speaking minister, complaining that their needs had been more neglected than if they had been American Indians, but reminding him that theirs was the ancient Scottish language and hoping that his expressed enthusiasm for Ossian would incline him to listen to them.[36] He ignored the petition, of course. In the end it was again Scott, aided in due course by Queen Victoria and the City of Glasgow Police Pipe Band, who made the Highland emblems (kilt, tartan, bagpipe) genuine pan-Scottish symbols. Only then was Scotland a coherently imagined community, and it helped that Gaelic speaking itself was in decline and could be ignored. Highland symbols were not Scottish symbols in the eighteenth century: the Highlands, then, were for most of the time a skeleton in the cupboard that patriots were far from anxious to parade.

To a degree, Dwyer's book complements Newman's. Newman is interested in how the luxury debate in England turns to a satirical and increasingly bitter criticism of cosmopolitanism and aristocracy, in how sensibility makes a cult of sincerity, and how the two fuse to form a powerful model for English or British national character. Dwyer is interested in how the luxury debate in Scotland becomes a criticism of the effects of modern commercial society on pristine national virtue— in effect a criticism of provincial *nouveaux riches*, not of aristocracy— and in how sensibility became the cult of a responsible gentleman preferring the sociability of neighbours, the scale of local activity and acts of private benevolence, to the false glory of acting on the metropolitan stage. Henry Mackenzie is important to both, *The Man of Feeling* at once a xenophobe hating foreign artificialities and a propagandist for the benevolent country landowner whose happiness lies in dwelling among the contented tenants of his own estate. However, many intellectual and political leaders in eighteenth-century Scotland enjoyed an indulgent sense of fulfilling their patriotic and civic duties while remaining completely conservative in their moral, religious and political views. The Moderate churchman Hugh Blair, for instance, thought himself every inch as much a Scot as Robert Burns (think of his rash and headstrong espousal of Macpherson's *Ossian*); while he was Burns' patron, and the ideal of a rustic bard of sensibility had profound appeal to him, he would have utterly deprecated Burns' levelling principles in the 1790s. More to his taste would have been the social view of his friend and colleague John Drysdale, who, in a sermon 'On the Distinction of Ranks', argued that the master-servant relationship was natural to society, that social levelling was inimical to the common interest, and that heaven, being a harmonious community, must itself be arranged in a fixed hierarchy of social rank like that on earth.[37]

Yet in a final analysis it is doubtful if the anti-modernising tradition of virtuous discourse had all the substantive importance that Dwyer imports to it. The ultimate victors were not conservatives who distrusted the rise of a commercial society and feared its social changes nor radicals who claimed universal civil rights partly for their own sake, partly as shields against the consequences of economic change. The victors were those who accepted commercial society as inevitable and welcome, though not unproblematical: Hume, whose view of luxury was that it could be beneficial to employment and economic growth,[38] the Smith of the *Wealth of Nations* rather than of the final revision of the *Theory of Moral Sentiments*, the merchants, the businessmen and above all the great army of rural improvers whose spokesman came to be Sir John Sinclair, and who certainly claimed to be patriots too.

There is danger of confusion here. Many landowning improvers fancied themselves in the rôle cast for them by the proponents of virtuous discourse, but few closely fitted that rôle in practice, judged by their behaviour. However they deluded themselves, they were out for profit rather than for benevolence. Nor did the rural improvers deserve all the credit for modernising Scotland that they claimed for themselves. Rather the point is that those who ultimately established an intellectual hegemony were those who believed that the highest good was the increase of 'national opulence'—that splendid eighteenth-century word, as superior to our 'economic growth' as 'astragal' is to 'double-glazing'. And nowhere was the hunt for opulence more closely allied to the language of patriotism than in the literature of rural improvement, where the self-interest of the improver and his country were constantly assumed to be identical. Truly one can quote here Victor Kiernan's remark about the eighteenth-century European landowning classes—'when such men "loved their country", they were thinking of it as a glorified private estate owned by themselves and their friends'.[39]

Only seldom was there overt, articulate protest against the assumption in late eighteenth-century Scotland that improvement was patriotic and its consequence universally benevolent. Tom Crawford has argued, and Andrew Noble agrees, that Burns' mouse, its nest upturned by the human's plough, was both itself and a symbol of man's own defencelessness against rural change:[40] but if this is true, both Burns' need to use coded language and his portrayal of the plough of change as being as unstoppable as fate are themselves revealing.

Sometimes in the debates carried on in the civil humanist mode among the *literati* there was hesitation about the direction that improvement was taking, most notably in the discussion of small *versus* large farms in the *Scots Magazine* of 1764, and the controversy over the law of entail which followed. Those who opposed reform argued that civic virtue and therefore both resistance to corrupting luxury and consideration to social inferiors resided naturally in the bosoms of an ancient nobility, but if they were once allowed freely to sell their lands, then Scotland would fall prey to commercial adventurers, nabobs and minor families seeking only luxury and self-enrichment at the expense of their tenants and neighbours.[41] But it was all rather contrived. Those in favour of entail reform argued in similar mode that virtue rested not with an overmighty and decadent feudal aristocracy, but with the middling landowners (a point with which Adam Smith would have agreed), and that they deserved the land. The notion that smaller gentry represented a virtuous antidote to aristocratic folly and vice was similarly put forward by John Millar and picked up as a weapon by the county freeholders in the 1780s. In any case the Scottish law of entail *was* reformed in the interest of raising capital on the security of land, which the Faculty of Advocates argued was essential if Scotland was to advance into the modern age, and an obstruction to untrammelled improvement was swept aside.

More basic and interesting, perhaps, were the criticisms aroused by the emigration mania which affected the Highlands and parts of the Lowlands round the west coast in the years 1769-1774—when the movement of perhaps as many as 20,000 people to Carolina and other parts of North America in the face of sustained rent-rises imposed by their landlords gave rise to the sharpest controversy of the eighteenth century as to the social benefits of agrarian change. It stirred Fergusson, in *A drink eclogue*, a jokey dialogue between a bottle of French brandy and one of Scotch whisky, where the whisky accused the brandy of corrupting the 'gentles':

   . . .for thee they hight their tenants rent,

And fill their lands wi' poortith, discontent:
Gar them o'er seas for cheaper mailins hunt,
An leave their ain as bare's the Cairn-o'-mount.

The two most interesting authors, though, both critical of the landed
classes and their assumptions, were William Thom, minister of Govan,
and William Ogilvie, professor of moral philosophy at the University of
Aberdeen.

Thom was the anonymous author of a pamphlet, *Candid inquiry into
the causes of the late and intended migrations from Scotland*, 1771, which
has some claims to be considered the first swallow in the summer of
Scottish radical writing.[42] Those who are leaving, he says, are not sturdy
beggars, or what was almost as bad, cooks, livery servants and
hairdressers, but 'chiefly sober industrious farmers . . .the most
useful and necessary hands in any country'. And the reason for the
drain in population is that 'in whatever country the whole property is
engrossed by a few, there the people must be wretched'. Scotland was a
country where the propertyless could scarcely ever acquire property,
and even when they did, they gained no new privilege or political
weight. 'In this part of the united kingdom, the democratical part of the
constitution, if it ever existed, is now nearly or altogether annihilated',
and far fewer in Scotland than England had a vote. Landlords pursue
measures which create misery by screwing up rents and shortening
leases until people would rather leave than stay. Simultaneously the
established clergy have 'endeavoured to explode the tenants' right to
possession by arguments so sutile and sophistical that I would blush to
mention them'. The fault, he says, is a political one arising from the fact
that the common people never had a sufficient check on the landholder:
'the political diseases of a state, and the vices which infeeble it or bring
on its decay, do commonly arise from its constitution'. Despite this
warm talk, I think unprecedented in Scotland until after the American
and French Revolutions, he sees no remedy but emigration: those who
want freedom and a future, he says, should get up and go. Thom is a
reminder that presbyterian ministers, even of the established church,
did not have to be as politically and socially conservative as the leaders
of the Moderates.

William Ogilvie seems to have gone to even greater trouble to conceal
his authorship of his *Essay on the right of property in land* (1781),
publishing it anonymously in London and evading every direct
reference to Scotland:[43] it is nevertheless directed against the
untrammelled rights of landowners, recommends emigration as one
solution for rural ills, and is clearly informed by the kind of situation he

saw around himself in Scotland from the 1760s onwards, when he had been an outspoken critic in the *Scots Magazine* of the increasing luxury of the landed classes.[44] Ogilvie was a genuine radical, albeit an inconsistent one: he based his views on the Rousseauean precept that all rights of property were founded either on occupancy or labour, that the earth had been given to mankind in common occupancy, and that every individual had a right by nature to possess and cultivate an equal share. 'This right is little different from that which he has to the free use of the open air and running water . . . [it] seems original, inherent and indefeasible . . . it is a birthright which every citizen still retains.'[45] This was the beginning of a powerful tract recognised as one of the earliest expressions of agrarian radicalism in English: in an ideal state fundamental laws should recognise 'the joint property of the whole community in the whole soil . . . which no possession of individuals, nor any industry by them applied to any portion of the soil, can ever cancel or impair'[46] (which sounds like Soviet collective farms); failing that he recommended rents fixed in perpetuity, perpetual leases, and tenancies converted into freeholds (very much like Irish and Highland land reforms from 1871 onwards). 'An unlimited property in land cannot be communicated to too great a number.' Of course, all this flies directly in the face of the free-market-in-land, improving ethic of eighteenth-century Britain. His inconsistencies spoiled the picture of an egalitarian, however, when he proposed the retention of feudal dues 'so regulated as to produce that degree of connection and dependence which may be expedient for preserving order and subordination.'[47] And, of course, his protests and proposals received no hearing whatsoever in his native country, which may even have been a relief to him.

In short, if we survey the intellectual protests against agrarian change in late eighteenth-century Scotland, there were few of them, and they were coded, weak or furtive. Nor did the protester indulge in the use of patriotic let alone nationalist rhetoric. Thom went so far as to recommend English law as superior to Scottish, and Ogilvie hid his Scottish identity completely. The improvers, on the other hand, steeped themselves from the beginning in the language of patriotism, which was implicit in the mode of discourse of civic humanism. Their improving societies were patriotic, from the Honourable Society of Improvers in 1723 to the Royal Society of Edinburgh and the Highland and Agricultural Society: all was for Scotland's greater good. Ultimately, getting rich was almost the same as being patriotic, as it is again today.

So where has this examination taken us? Three tentative conclusions could be drawn. Firstly, Scottish feelings of national identity in the eighteenth century were strong and powerful, but they were not, except under abnormal and temporary provocation, anti-English. Rather they were of the 'concentric loyalty' type which tended rather to reinforce British nationalism than to contradict it: if Scots identified an external foe at all, it was France, and then only in wartime. Under extreme patriotic stress even a Francophile and cosmopolitan intellectual like Adam Smith joined his friends Alexander Carlyle, John Home and Adam Ferguson in an Anti-Gallican Society in 1780.[48] By and large, however, the Scots were conscious of no natural enemies, and thus failed the first test for developing nationalism. Even when intellectuals were humiliated by English condescension and, worse, it failed to overwhelm their genuine feelings of loyalty to a greater Britain.

Second, most radicals of the 1790s shared this concentric loyalty with everyone else: they wished to attain democracy through realising Cartwright's patriotic vision, but their method envisaged Scotland inheriting through the Union a democratic English past, and hoping by modern energy, strengthened by recollection of epochs of resistance to tyranny in her own history, to recover British Liberty for all the British people. One might have imagined that a class critique, as it slowly emerged between Tom Paine and the Charter, would be accompanied by a nationalist critique along the lines of fight the upper classes, fight the Anglicised, fight the English—but it never did.

Thirdly, and perhaps decisively, the language of patriotism was nowhere used more persistently than by the improvers in describing and legitimating their own pursuit of opulence. Their occupation of this lofty ground was one of several reasons why it was so hard to overturn the hegemony of the twin ideas that national enrichment was synonymous with patriotism, and that national enrichment was best attained by allowing the upper classes a free hand in the pursuit of wealth. It was as though the Invisible Hand belonged to an Englishman with a sharp set of Scottish fingernails.[49]

NOTES

1. T. Nairn, *The Break-up of Britain* (London, 1977), esp. pp.96-108.
2. A.D. Smith, *The Ethnic Revival* (London, 1981), pp.37-42.
3. *Ibid.*, pp.55, 164ff.
4. J.C.D. Clark, *Revolution and Rebellion: State and Society in England in the Seventeenth and Eighteenth Centuries* (Cambridge, 1986), p.102.
5. Gerald Newman, *The Rise of English Nationalism: a Cultural History 1740-1830*

(London, 1987), pp.53, 163.

6.   J.A. Smith. 'Some eighteenth-century ideas of Scotland', in N.T. Phillipson and R. Mitchison, eds. *Scotland in the Age of Improvement: Essays in Scottish History in the Eighteenth Century* (Edinburgh, 1970), pp.107-124.

7.   H.W. Meikle, *Scotland and the French Revolution* (Glasgow, 1912), pp.174-6.

8.   J.D. Brims, 'The Scottish "Jacobins", Scottish nationalism and British Union', in R. Mason (ed.), *Scotland and England, 1786-1815* (Edinburgh, 1987), pp.247-265.

9.   K.J. Logue, *Popular Disturbances in Scotland, 1780-1815* (Edinburgh, 1979), p.111.

10.   [Earl of Cromarty], *Parainesis pacifica: or a persuasive to the Union of Britain* (London, 1702), p.4; I.G. Brown, 'Modern Rome and ancient Caledonia: the Union and the politics of Scottish culture', in A. Hook, ed. *The History of Scottish Literature*, in Vol 2, *1660-1800* (Aberdeen, 1987), pp.33-50.

11.   J. Robertson, *Scottish Enlightenment and the Militia Issue* (Edinburgh, 1985), pp.237-8.

12.   For example, in *An expedition to Fife*, and *Fashion*.

13.   *Edinburgh Review*, 1755-6, preface.

14.   Robertson, *Militia Issue*.

15.   *Report of the Royal Commission on the Laws of Marriage*, pp.11867-8, xxxii, Appendix p.77.

16.   N.T. Phillipson, 'Scottish public opinion and the Union in the age of association', in Phillipson and Mitchison, *Age of Improvement*, pp.125-147.

17.   Quoted in J.A. Smith, 'Some eighteenth-century ideas', p.109.

18.   Henry Mackenzie, *The Man of Feeling* (edn. Cupar, Fife, 1803), p.47.

19.   Quoted in J.A. Smith, 'Some eighteenth-century ideas', p.113.

20.   Isaiah Berlin, *Against the Current: Essays in the History of Ideas* (New York, 1980), p.346.

21.   G. Turnbull, 'James Boswell: biography and the Union', in Hook, *History of Scottish Literature*, Vol. 2, pp.157-174.

22.   Newman, *Nationalism*, pp.152-3.

23.   H.M. Atherton, *Political Prints in the Age of Hogarth* (Oxford, 1974).

24.   J.A. Smith, 'Some eighteenth-century ideas', p.109.

25.   Newman, *Nationalism*, pp.68-9, 133-5.

26.   J. Cartwright, *Take your choice!* (London, 1776).

27.   Brims, 'The Scottish "Jacobins" ', p.252.

28.   Peter Mackenzie, *The Life of Thomas Muir* (Glasgow, 1831), pp.95-6.

29   *The Edinburgh Gazetteer*, 24 December 1793. I am grateful to John Brims for this reference.

30.   J.D. Brims, 'The Covenanting tradition and Scottish radicalism in the 1790s', unpublished paper presented at the symposium on 'Dissent, protest and rebellion in pre-industrial Scotland', Association of Scottish Historical Studies, 1987; T.C. Smout, *A Century of the Scottish People, 1830-1950* (London, 1986), pp.236-8.

31.   J.D. Young, *The Rousing of the Scottish Working Class* (London, 1979), p.59.

32.   Robertson, *Militia Issue*; J. Dwyer, *Virtuous Discourse: Sensibility and Community in Late Eighteenth-Century Scotland* (Edinburgh, 1987).

33.   Dwyer, *Virtuous Discourse*, p.39.

34.   B. Anderson, *Imagined Communities: Reflections on the Origin and Spread of Nationalism* (London, 1983).

35.   I am indebted to my colleague Roger Mason for pointing this out to me.

36.   Alexander Murdoch drew my attention to this. SRO CH.2/47/6, Caithness

Presbytery minutes, 1799-1818, folios 209-11.

37. Dwyer, *Virtuous Discourse*, p.22.

38. J. Hoppit, 'The Luxury debate in Britain, 1660-1790', unpublished paper presented at the workshop on 'The luxury trades and early industrialisation', Victoria and Albert Museum, London, 1987, pp.8-9.

39. V. Kiernan, 'Nationalist movements and social classes', in A.D. Smith (ed.), *Nationalist Movements* (London, 1976).

40. A. Noble, 'Dissent in the Englightenment', unpublished paper presented at the symposium on 'Dissent', Association of Scottish Historical Studies, p.24.

41. Dwyer, *Virtuous Discourse*, pp.41-2; Phillipson, 'Public opinion and the union', pp.141-2.

42. [Anon.], *Candid inquiry into the causes of the late and intended migrations from Scotland* (Glasgow, n.d.). Internal evidence shows that it dates from 1771. See especially pp.1-2, 10-11, 14-16, 41, 57.

43. William Ogilvie, *Essay on the right of property in land* (London, 1781).

44. Dwyer, *Virtuous Discourse*, p.105 - but he fails to identify his later interests in land reform.

45. Ogilvie, *Essays*, pp.1-3.

46. *Ibid.*, p.62.

47. *Ibid.*, p.154.

48. Robertson, *Militia Issue*, p.137.

49. This paper has been greatly improved by the comments and suggestions of my colleagues John Brims and Roger Mason, though neither would necessarily approve of the content and drift of its argument.

2

James Boswell: Scotland's Prodigal Son

Andrew Noble

There's nae hope for Jamie, mon . . .Jamie is gane clean gyte. What do you think, mon? He's done wi' Paoli—he's off wi' the land-louping scoundrel of a Corsican: and whose tail do you think he has pinned himself to now, mon? . . .A *dominie,* mon—an auld dominie! he keeped a schule, and caud it an acaadamy.[1]

As far as Lord Auchinleck was concerned the story of his prodigal son was not to have a happy ending. This paternal denunciation, perhaps intensified by a hurt sense of his son's pursuit of surrogate fathers, is in style and substance intensely Scottish. We are a factual, reductive people; the deflation of pretension we count not the least of our virtues. Such pride, however, can come before an imaginative fall. Auchinleck's judgemental vision of his son, paradigm of so much of Scotland's response to creativity, had so intense a vision of an unstable reprobate that it utterly missed the essential fact that what he had sired was a genius.

Every time I visit our university library I receive sad, salutary testimony to the long-term consequences of James Boswell's rootless, restless life. Strathclyde's Scottish literature shelves are well stocked. Boswell has, however, either been dismissed the service or broken ranks. The magisterial volumes of the magnificent, ongoing Yale edition are on parade in the English literature section. The Scottish literary tradition, one of extremely erratic achievement, can hardly afford to do without Boswell's contribution. Exposing himself to the diverse, often dangerous currents of the Enlightenment, undoubtedly among the most stylish and formally innovative of the great European prose writers of that age, Boswell's reputation, however, still rests more on American scholarship than Scottish recognition.[2] In a properly laudatory review of Frank Brady's recent biography, *James Boswell: The Later Years 1769-1795*, Tom Crawford has bitterly commented on this sorry situation:

When will we establish him securely in the canon as one of the very greatest writers to have been born in Scotland; when, for example, will his name be there at Prestwick airport to greet transatlantic visitors among those of other Scottish luminaries; when under the influence of Macaulay, the hero-worshippers and the unco guid, will we stop being ashamed of him.[3]

Certainly, like his fellow randy Ayrshire genius, Burns, Boswell has been the victim of Scottish puritan-inspired gentility. Unlike Burns, however, other more serious charges have been laid at his door. His snobbery is alleged to have amounted to treason against his native land. His appetite for Johnson's London as opposed to his aversion to Hume's Edinburgh, an Edinburgh at the very zenith of its intellectual powers, seems absurd and perverse. Ironically, it is Crawford himself who takes Brady to task for letting Boswell off this particular hook:

One defect of *The Later Years* has already been pointed out by David Daiches—that Brady, for all his profound knowledge of eighteenth-century Scotland, appears to take Boswell's opinion of it at face-value, as a second-rate provincial backwater with a second-rate intellectual life. Andrew Noble takes Boswell's (and Brady's?) view even further: for Noble Boswell is the archetypal Scottish writer who 'went South not for foreign gold but to receive an imaginative succour no longer possible in Scotland's prissy cultural capital . . . . . Even at the height of the Enlightenment, Boswell found it not a creatively stimulating place.'[4]

On the face of it, Crawford's charge seems overwhelmingly true. Indeed as we Scots read the most recently published of his journals, *The English Experiment 1785-1789,* we are caught between sorrow and outrage as his life falls apart in futile, sycophantic attempts to secure an English political or legal career. Indeed the more he is rebuffed, the more he craves not only English preferment but style not only for himself but his children: 'Were my daughters to be Edinburgh-mannered girls, I could have no satisfaction in their company'.[5] He is, indeed, towards the end, a truly displaced person, self-deprived of career prospects on either side of the Border:

I was not only disappointed in any views of ambition in the wide sphere of London, but from my having addicted myself almost entirely to English Society, and my aversion to Scotch manners and contempt of provincial consequence being known, I had too much reason to apprehend that should I apply for the office of Lord of Session, I should not be able to obtain it. I was in truth in a woeful state of depression in every respect.[6]

Playing aspirant mouse to the Earl of Lonsdale's cat, trudging through the Cumbrian snow away from and then back to his tyrannical English master's bleak, freezing castle, there are few more pathetic and less elevating sights than this self-unmaking Scotsman. How typical of Boswell, perhaps even of the Scottish temperament, that in the disintegration of his ambitious cravings he should simultaneously be writing one of the greatest books in the language, his life of Dr. Johnson. Such an astonishing fact should, then, give us pause before we embark on too facile condemnation of Boswell's antipathy to Edinburgh and his belief that in London lay the stimulating key to his creativity. At a superficial level he can be defined as a neurotic chameleon attracted by the most liverish colours of worldly ambition. Having early tasted the social, intellectual, fleshly delights of London, Edinburgh grew increasingly sour on his tongue. His unstable personality was beset by a host of Edinburgh-inspired psychosomatic illnesses stemming from domestic boredom, professional restraint and the lack of not intellectual but *creative* writers of a stature comparable to his own. His unfortunate wife had to deal with a caged lion in their New Town flat. His response to London was one of reactive mania; his year was compulsively shaped round the annual jaunt south. 'My wife', he writes, 'disliked Fielding's turn for low life . . . . But it is human nature. She has nothing of that English juiciness of mind of which I have a great deal, which makes me delight in humour.'[7] As Brady has pointed out, Edinburgh, unlike London, gave Boswell no fertile ground. On the one hand he felt himself grow dissolute and vulgar among its seamy hard-drinkers; on the other he felt constrained by its prim, insipid provincialism.

Underlying such social restraints lay deeper, more painful forms of authority: his lawyer father and a judgemental Presbyterianism brooded over him. Sabbatarian Edinburgh provided for Boswell the dark night of his soul. Protestant Holland in 1763 brought it all painfully back to him:

> Th' approach of Sunday still I can't but dread,
> For still old Edinburgh comes into my head,
> Where on that day a dreary gloom appears,
> And the kirk-bells ring doleful in your ears.
> Enthusiasts sad, how can you thus employ
> What your Redeemer made a day of joy?
> With thankful hearts to your Creator pray,
> From labour rest, be cheerful and be gay.
> Let us not keep the Sabbath of the Jews;
> Let generous Christians Christian freedom use.[8]

Edinburgh was a city where priests in black gowns were perpetually binding with thorns Boswell's joys and desires. Often his promiscuity seems not so much the brutal functioning of eighteenth-centry upper-class masculinity, a thing of amoral, nocturnal thrusts, as providing occasion for Calvinist-inspired guilt and abasement. Again, it was Holland which evoked lust, compassion, guilt and resentment in our hyper-Scottish lad of enlarged parts:

> At five I went to a bawdy-house. I was shown upstairs and had a bottle of claret and a *juffrow*. But the girl was much fitter for being wrapped in the blankets of salvation than kissed between the sheets of love. I had no armour, so did not fight. It was truly ludicrous to talk in Dutch to a whore. The scene was to me a rarity as great as peas in February. Yet I was hurt to find myself in the sinks of great debauchery. This was a proper way to consider the thing. But so sickly was my brain that I had the low scruples of an Edinburgh divine.[9]

We are here reminded of the flights of Joyce and Beckett from what they felt were restraints of Dublin's priest-ridden society. It has been argued, recently and lucidly, that the contribution of the moderate clergy to eighteenth-century Scotland represents a finely balanced cultural triumph. Boswell conceived of their virtuous discourses as, however, at best hypocritical. A liberal theatre for Boswell could never truly emerge from the sermon's monologue. At worst he thought that only a veneer had been placed on Calvinism. What we must try and distinguish in this situation is, I think, that what to the historian of culture is an extraordinary, even unique, phenomenon, is not necessarily the same thing as what is necessary to the stuff of creative literature. No great art has emerged from genteel, sentimental and theoretically benevolent literature. Much censorious and destructive criticism has. Edwin Muir's account of post-Calvinist Edinburgh's culture is impressionistic but, an utterly different personality from Boswell, he shares the latter's hostility stemming as it does from a sense of a creatively hurtful national environment.[10]

Boswell could no more accept sentimental, genteel restraint in his personal behaviour than he could in literary terms. On an emotional switchback, he was consistent only in his inconsistencies. Characteristic of divided Scottish siblings, his brother David tried in 1767 to dampen the disruptive 'Vanity and Self-Conceit' resulting from his Corsican political and literary triumph. 'The people of Edinburgh in general are now beginning to look upon you,' he wrote, 'as a man like Lord Kames who does the most extravagant things without thought or reflection.'[11] In that same year David Hume described him to the Comtesse de Boufflers as 'very good humoured, very agreeable and very mad'.[12] Hume, having theoretically dispersed a coherent self or soul, was perhaps disturbed at perceiving before him a creature who could indeed behave as if composed of discrete, hence unstable, sensory impressions. On his side, Boswell craved the coherence of what he believed were lost secular and spiritual orders. His anxiety about immortality can perhaps be gauged as being in direct proportion to his need to press and penetrate female flesh. Only someone so demented by terminal doubt and fear could also have been driven to transcribe the maximum possible amount of experience into text. 'Yet,' he wrote, 'I have certainly much more of *myself* thus preserved than most people have.'[13] He and Swift (another writer not favoured in nor favouring Edinburgh) are both obsessed with the same problem, the dark, hidden side of the Enlightenment's secular and scientific optimism, the consequences of the self as only finite organism. They are, of course, wholly different in their formal dramatisations of the dilemma. Boswell is personal and biographical where Swift is impersonal and political.[14]

Like Swift he, too, yearned for a return to a supposedly lost conservative order; his Catholicism was deeper than the manifest attraction for him of aesthetic ritual. It was also, of course, another affront to throw in the face of his whig, presbyterian father. Moderate, prudent, professionally successful as a judge and secure as an aristocratic landowner, Auchinleck was a father figure inducing the most intense love and hate in the son. He simultaneously yearned for and reacted against his father's stable values and virtues; values and virtues of prudence and moderation which were essentially those of the Edinburgh Enlightenment.

Siding with his put-down, religious mother, Boswell nevertheless spent his life up to early middle age simultaneously contending with his father and trying to seek his approval. He spent over forty years preparing to play his father's legal and landholding role. He was, when he did finally succeed him, a disastrous flop.

His paternal struggles are replete with that uniquely Boswellian medium of farce combined with Freudian nightmare. He himself led the nocturnal pro-Douglas mob to break his father's windows. On Boswell's marrying his impoverished cousin quite against his father's wishes, his father struck back by getting married in Edinburgh to *his* first cousin on the same day as his son tied the knot in Ayrshire! For James having to plead in court with papa on the bench must have seemed like a terrible premonition of Calvinism's last judgement. Little wonder that, like Burns, Byron and Stevenson, he was prone to bouts of depression in which he envisaged himself as impotent and eternally damned. He is akin to a bloated extrovert playing Kafka.

Indeed, in the intensity and frequency of its oedipal struggles it could be argued that so much of subsequent Scottish fictional art imitates Boswell's life. Scott's fiction is replete with this theme. In *Redgauntlet*, indeed, the strife between father and son becomes the motivating force of the family and implicitly the nation's history. Scott sought an end to these quarrels, but subsequent Scottish fiction has near-obsessively replayed the drama of the conservative, authoritarian father enraged by the impotently radical, artistic son, rendered effeminate by proximity to his mother. Hence we have *Gillespie*, *The House with the Green Shutters* and, most clearly and painfully, R.L. Stevenson's *Weir of Hermiston*.

Stevenson, whom Henry James described as having 'the filial relation quite classically troubled',[15] was from an early age acutely aware of Boswell. As the apprentice writer he wrote to Mrs Sitwell in 1876 that he read 'Boswell daily by way of a Bible: I mean to read Boswell now until the day I die'.[16] In part this is one stylist of genius responding to an ancestral other, but Stevenson must have seen in Boswell's paternal struggles a mirror image of his own. It is thus no accident that in *Weir* Archie's father is a judge, that in Lord Glenalmond we find Archie seeking the consolation that in real life Boswell sought from Lord Kames or that the son is so agonised by legal power which led to public execution.

For Boswell and Stevenson Edinburgh was the undermining city of their authoritarian fathers. 'He had,' Stevenson wrote in the preface to *The Master of Ballantrae*, 'already almost forgiven himself his two unpardonable errors, that he should never have left his native city or that he should have ever returned to it.'[17] The covert literary battle fought out in Edinburgh in the century after the Union was, however, no joke. In linguistic terms it expressed itself in the desire of the prospering anglicised middle class to cast off their dialect by purgation of their Scotticisms. It is wholly characteristic of Boswell that he should hold two utterly different points of view on this. His journals, especially when in England, are peppered with irascible comments on the manner in which Scottish accents and vocabulary grate on the refined ear. In 1773 Johnson praised him as the '*most unscottified*' of his countrymen. One of his earliest rôle and voice models was that supreme elocutionist of the Edinburgh scene, the Irishman, Sheridan. At the same time Boswell brooded for years over the compilation of a Scottish dictionary.

What sort of dictionary this would have made or what sort of writer Boswell would have been working in his native medium can only be speculated.[18] Never more than a spasmodic, journeyman poet, there is, however, evidence to suggest that a Scottish vocabulary gave in his verse an edge and specificity quite lacking in his English productions. For example, as Fredrick Pottle has demonstrated, his English and Scottish verse responses to the Douglas case are markedly different:

> No birth must henceforth be believ'd
>   Unless proclaim'd by sound of trumpet,
> And ev'ry dame of high degree
>   Become as brazen as a strumpet . . . .

To which we can compare these lines which, revealingly, existed in his own lifetime only in a private letter:

> French proofs! Howt, man, gae haud your tongue!
> For to sic proofs nae judge e'er lippens;
> Gowpins O' gowd your cause has cost
> And after aw it's no worth tippence.[19]

There is no doubt that inherent in Scottish vocabulary there is, as MacDiarmid has frequently stated, a factuality that is not only precise but frequently irreverent and reductive. Scottish poetry is capable of both exquisitely understated lyricism and powerful satire. Boswell, on occasion, could switch on this latter abrasive, ironic power. Hence in conversation with Rousseau he makes a mental note that:

> It was just as if I had said, "Hoot, Johnie Rousseau man, what for hae ye sae mony figmagairies? Ye're a bony man indeed to mak siccan a wark; set ye up. Canna ye just live like ither fowk".[20]

For the anglicising Edinburgh middle class, whose menfolk could lapse into private, playful, regressive use of native speech, such a deflationary, dissenting public language would have been quite incompatible with their social ambitions and political aims. The resultant tensions in eighteenth-century Scottish poetics are consequently extremely complex. Three poets of ascending genius, Ramsay, Fergusson and Burns, combined vernacular language with not only recovered native forms but also sophisticated borrowings from contemporary English poetry. Inherent in such language and form is a repudiation of the loss of an ethnic culture and political freedom implicit in the Union and a protest about the agrarian distress caused by the improving methods of the new economics.[21] This protest culminates in Burns who, energised by a vision of international revolution, devised brilliant, often necessarily covert, strategies of satirical dissent.

Hence from mid-century onwards Edinburgh becomes a cockpit for literary critical battles as the genteel, sentimental and censorious literati attempted to suppress the irreverent, inspired voices of native protest. Their main response was to impose a stereotype of false pastoralism; nothing was more compatible with their political aspirations than the image of a placid, contented, thrifty peasantry. When this failed, rougher tactics were resorted to. Consider, for example, Henry Mackenzie's treatment of Fergusson. Consider, too, the restricting condescension which Burns suffered in Edinburgh and which Carol MacGuirk has recently and finely discussed.[22] As Edwin Muir remarked of Burns and Edinburgh:

> His fame and his journey to Edinburgh again enveloped him in the stupendous Scots respectability of that time; the elegant and priggish minister Blair, the virtuous and respectable Dugald Stewart, the historian Robertson sat beside him wondering visibly whether their young genius would become a really respected poet and a prosperous and godly farmer. Their society must occasionally have appeared to him like the reading of an interminable dull tract.

> But indeed his educated friends, except for one or two women, had only virtue to recommend them, while his boon companions were equally without sense and sensibility. In spite of a lifelong desire for friends, he found only moralists and tipplers; and although he could move these by the astonishing spectacle of his thoughts and passions, so that when he spoke from his heart they wept, he received nothing back from them to give him happiness, nor, except in states of drunken effusion, any direct human comprehension. As his life grew poorer he returned to these states more and more rather than to the intelligent men of virtue who had less than nothing to give him and gave grudgingly[23]

Muir's vision of an Edinburgh polarised into a city of 'moralists and tipplers' with the writer finding no energising, creative middle ground accords closely to Boswell's derogatory diagnosis. Burns wrote an admiring but unanswered letter to Boswell.[24] It would be naive in the extreme, however, to imagine Boswell befriending him. Boswell, at a conscious level, was a social snob fantasising about a hierarchical society in which his gross instability was given the secure position for which it yearned. Subconsciously, he was a political anarchist who occasionally ran amok. Dr Johnson and John Wilkes were accordingly models for his antipathetic political selves. At a creative level, a level which renders his manifest absurdities and follies irrelevant, he was an embracer of problematic reality, an eighteenth-century James Joyce, who found decorous, genteel conventions intolerable. As Frank Brady remarks of the Mediterranean-travelling Boswell of 1765:

> James Boswell's main concerns during the period of his life covered by this volume were sex, religion, and politics—the three subjects of conversation forbidden in polite society. To be sure, these essential interests occupied his mind a great deal throughout his life, as they do most men's; where he differed from others was in the determination with which he explored them both in words and action, and in the frankness and relish for detail with which he set down not only

conversations, but also his feelings and his experiences in general. This is not a polite book, because Boswell insisted on asking fundamental questions both of himself and of others—a trait that some have found indelicate, but which accounts in part for the warm response he evoked from such varied and distinguished men as Rousseau, Paoli and Dr Johnson.[25]

Given that wholly complete and exact cultural parallels cannot exist, it is revealing to compare the situation of Boswell to that of another great, even more insurrectionary genius, Herman Melville. In the middle of the nineteenth century Melville felt both his own nascent genius and that of his nation trapped by the hegemony of anglicised Boston. 'Let us,' he wrote, 'away with Bostonian leaven of literary flunkeyism towards England.'[26] Eager for a more virile, realistic art that spoke to the condition and anticipations of this new society, he sought to release American artists from their provincial New England prison. Not to do so was to live a contradiction in terms, imitative creative lives. It was also to create a literary climate, provincial in the worst sense, where second-hand goods achieved the highest applause and rewards. Melville's description of Washington Irving would fit not a few of Edinburgh's post-union literary luminaries:

> But that graceful writer who perhaps of all Americans has received the most plaudits from his own country for his productions—that very popular and amiable writer, however good, and self-reliant in many things, perhaps owes his chief reputation to the self-acknowledged imitation of a foreign model and to the studied avoidance of all topics but smooth ones. But it is better to fail in originality than to succeed in imitation.[27]

It is not certain whether Melville believed that a literary nationalism could function without a literary capital. Arguably America has never achieved such a city. American writers who stayed at home have often led a life defined by Saul Bellow as akin to that of the gopher. The many great American literary expatriates who fled populist America in search of a cosmopolitan tradition in what they believed were the great, sacred art capitals of Europe considered that the requisite conditions for major art were not present in their own country. In a review of *Scottish Literature: Character and Influence* by G. Gregory Smith written in 1919 T.S. Eliot, at the beginning of both his long exile and his deviant Englishness, perceived parallels between his predicament and that of the Scots who, fleeing their provincialism, had been drawn by London's creatively magnetic force:

> . . . . . Edinburgh literature was important *provincial* literature about 1800. The

last is not the importance of a separate literature; it is the importance of a provincial capital which at a certain time happens to contain as many or more men of importance than the metropolis. Edinburgh, in 1800, of which Mr Gregory Smith gives a pleasing glimpse, is analogous to Boston in America fifty years later. It was as interesting, perhaps for a moment more interesting than London. But a provincial capital, even with the *Edinburgh* and *Blackwood's* of a hundred years ago, is the matter of a moment; it depends on the continuous supply of important men; the instant the supply falls off, the metropolis, even if suffering from a poverty, gains the ascendant. And then the important men turn to the metropolis.[28]

Post-1800 it is Carlyle, departing Edinburgh with cries of execration against what he claimed were the restrictions and French-inspired sceptical superficialities of its culture and university, who provides the most telling Scottish paradigm of Eliot's London thesis. Granting all his excesses and inconsistencies, is a social critical voice of Carlyle's virulence and stature imaginable as emanating from nineteenth-century Edinburgh?[29] One aspect of Carlyle's unlikely admiration for Boswell may have lain in his sympathy with the latter's prior acceptance of the reality of London as the essential locus for the Scottish writer. Writing to a London newspaper in 1779, Boswell said that Scotland had been deprived of 'all national dignity' and 'all the advantages of its own parliament'. 'London', he wrote, 'is now the metropolis of the whole island, the grand emporium of everything valuable, the strong centre of attraction for all of us.'[30]

At this point Boswell can be defined as either the ultimate Scottish literary traitor or a genius who had metamorphosed himself from mere provincial into major English writer. The truth is more complex. If, in terms of practical advantage, what 'concentric loyalty' offered to the Scottish commercial, aristocratic and professional classes was highly desirable, it led Scottish writers into profound anxieties about their identity and literary purposes. Scottish poetry went into different national directions. James Thompson wrote 'Rule Britannia'; Robert Fergusson wrote 'The Ghaists'. Scottish fiction, with Scott, presented novels which, only superficially Scottish, were in reality a renunciation of the turbulence of Scottish history and tradition and celebrations of the security and wealth provided by the Union.

Boswell, characteristically, was pulled in both directions. Emotionally he was pro-Jacobite. He had no small sense of his lineage; he was proud of his ancestor Thomas Boswell who 'was killed at Flodden Field fighting with his king against the English, for Scotland and England were then two kingdoms'.[31] He refused to visit John Wilkes in prison because 'I am a Scotch laird and a Scotch lawyer and a Scotch married man. It would not be decent'.[32] Would that being 'a Scotch married man' had been for Boswell a constant antidote to indecency. Perhaps the most comic and revealing image of Boswell's confused sense of national identity is to be found in his Corsican journal:

> The *ambisciatore inglese,* as the good peasants and soldiers used to call me, became a great favourite among them. I got a Corsican dress made, in which I walked about with an air of true satisfaction . . . . One day they would needs hear me play upon my German flute. To have told my honest visitants, "Really, gentlemen, I play very ill", and put on such airs as we do in our genteel companies, would have been highly ridiculous. I therefore immediately complied with their request. I gave them one or two Italian airs, and then some of our beautiful old Scots tunes: "Gilderoy", "The Lass of Patie's Mill", "Corn rigs are bonny". The pathetic simplicity and pastoral gaiety of the Scots music will always please those who have the genuine feelings of nature. The Corsicans were charmed with the specimens I gave them, though I may now say they were very indifferently performed.
>
> My good friends insisted also to have an English song from me. I endeavoured to please them in this too, and was very lucky in that which occurred to me. I sung them "Hearts of oak are our ships, Hearts of oak are our men." I translated it into Italian for them, and never did I see men so delighted with a song as the Corsicans were with the *Hearts of Oak*. "Cuore di quercia," cried they, "bravo Inglese!" It was quite a joyous riot. I fancied myself to be a recruiting sea officer. I fancied all my chorus of Corsicans aboard the British fleet.[33]

The linguistic and musical versatility, the metamorphoses of social and national identities are here so compellingly, histrionically comic that one almost wishes that Richard Poirier's thesis that the essence of art is not tradition but transient performance were credible. Like his fellow Scots, however, tradition stirred uneasily in Boswell's dreams to the extent that a Paoli-inspired Corsica becomes a subconscious surrogate for a denationalised, lost Scotland. Boswell as inspirational rhetorician is at least as successful with the natives as in his role of performing artist:

> At Bastelica, where there is a stately, spirited race of people, I had a large company to attend me in the convent. I liked to see their natural frankness and ease, for why should men be afraid of their own species? They just came in, making an easy bow, placed themselves round the room where I was sitting, rested themselves on their muskets, and immediately entered into conversation with me. They talked very feelingly of the miseries that their country had endured, and complained that they were still but in a state of poverty. I happened at that time to have an unusual flow of spirits, and as one who finds himself amongst utter strangers in a distant country has no timidity, I harangued the men of Bastelica with great fluency. I expatiated on the bravery of the Corsicans by which they had purchased liberty,

the most valuable of all possessions, and rendered themselves glorious over all Europe. Their poverty, I told them, might be remedied by a proper cultivation of their island and by engaging a little in commerce. But I bid them remember that they were much happier in their present state than in a state of refinement and vice, and that therefore they should beware of luxury.[34]

Quite what the brave Corsicans made of this polemical mixture of Rousseau and the moral economics of the Scottish Enlightenment is not certain. More seriously revealing is the stress on the sustenance among them of invaluable liberty and that this essential matter was more easily spoken of not at home but among strangers. Was Byron also acting out in his Greek tragedy a similar freedom-seeking caused by displaced national identity? Since the Union Scottish writing has been haunted by a sense of not only lost political but, indeed, spiritual liberty. In the eighteenth century a minority issued a poetic call to arms. Lesser writers sold out for English literary gold. Others fabricated compensatory fantasies and two, Boswell and Scott, attempted to imaginatively endorse the Union and celebrate a Scottish identity not so much surrendered as metamorphosed into a greater whole.

What we can perceive in the wake of the Union is a struggle going on in Scottish creative consciousness to establish a specific, underlying myth which would render Scottish history an acceptable, intelligible story. The highest achievement in this field has been MacDiarmid's inevitably ambivalent *A Drunk Man Looks at the Thistle*. In the eighteenth century this search for a myth explains the excitement over Wilkie's *Epigoniad* and MacPherson's *Ossian*. This stemmed from a desire to swing things in an ethnic rather than a literary balance. Melville is again highly relevant here in his anglophobic analysis of mid-nineteenth century American writing:

Let America then prize and cherish her writers; yea let her glorify them. They are not so many in number as to exhaust her good will. And while she has good kith and kin of her own, to take to her bosom, let her not lavish her embraces upon the household of an alien. For believe it or not, England, after all, is, in many things, an alien to us. China has more bowels of real love for us than she. But even were there no strong literary individualities among us, as there are some dozen at least, nevertheless, let America first praise mediocrity, even in her own children, before she praises (for everywhere, merit demands acknowledgement from everyone) the best excellence in the children of any other land. Let her own authors, I say, have the priority of appreciation. I was much pleased with a hot-headed Carolina cousin of mine, who once said, "If there were no other American to stand by, in Literature—why, then, I would stand by Pop Emmons and his *Fredoniad*, and till a better epic came along, swear it was not very far behind the *Iliad*." Take away the words, and in spirit he was sound.[35]

The danger, so frequently manifest in Scotland, is, of course, that this sort of literary nationalism leads precisely to a literal interpretation. Even more dangerous, as the pseudo-Homeric fantasies of the literati demonstrate, is that the fevered dreams of a sickly, impotent nationalism will almost inevitably seek succour in an allegedly exclusive lost past. This is often a sinister twilight world populated by figures of militaristic fantasy. Post-Union Scotland, progressive, moderate Scotland, dreams strange dreams; dreams which seem often compensatory fantasies for the trauma of national emasculation. How else can one explain Lowland Scotland's absorption since 1745 in the image of the martial Highlander?

Boswell shared this absorption. In his best travel book, *Journal of a Tour to the Hebrides*, we find perhaps the single most revealing statement of the tug of the Highlander on the Lowland Scottish sensibility:

> McQueen walked some miles to give us a convoy. He had, in 1745, joined the Highland army at Fort Augustus, and continued in it till after the battle of Culloden. As he narrated the particulars of that ill-advised, but brave attempt, I could not refrain from tears. There is a certain association of ideas in my mind upon that subject, by which I am strongly affected. The very Highland names, or the sound of a bag-pipe, will stir my blood, and fill me with a mixture of melancholy and respect for courage; with a pity for unfortunate and superstitious regard for antiquity, and thoughtless inclination for war; in short with a crowd of sensation with which sober rationality had nothing to do.[36]

The temptation for the Lowland Scot to see in the tragedy of the Highlands an image of national disaster was not only self-indulgent but corrosive of a genuine nationalism. The least of its perils is that it provides Lord Dacre, in converting so much of subsequent Scottish history into an impotent tartan pageant, with so much knowing fun.[37] This pseudo-mythical Highlands existed for many Scots as either an image of irretrievable loss, or even more dangerously, as an energy that would resurrect itself and purge the nation of its national and creative enervation. Hence, for example, mingled with MacDiarmid's vision of a Marxist future we find atavistic fantasies of Celtic resurrection.[38]

What these fantasies also provided a tribe of Scottish writers with was a body of irrational sensation which was in the cosmopolitan, middle-brow market place extremely profitable. To this Boswell never succumbed. He was saved from sentimental exploitation of the Highlands both by the fidelity of his documentary impulses and Johnson's presence. Johnson brought to his *Journey to the Western Islands* his unwavering curiosity for social detail and how things actually worked. As a man of the Enlightenment he had, albeit highly qualified, a belief in universal progress. Yet the suppressed, melancholic side of his nature senses a social tragedy. In the wake of Culloden, he feared that Highland life was irretrievably damaged. On the one hand he saw the gradual incorporation of the Highlander into the prospering mainstream of the nation's economic life. On the other hand he thought that the combination of governmental injustice regarding weapons and costume after the '45 combined with the fact their chiefs would 'gradually degenerate from patriarchal rulers to rapacious landlords' would depopulate the Highlands. He saw a society trapped in a limbo between decrepit feudalism and nascent capitalism. Both he and Boswell in their conservative hearts were deeply depressed by the decline of feudalism's paternal responsibilities. Thus the major destructive force which stalked the Highlands in 1773 was *voluntary* emigration: 'In the *Hebrides*, the loss of an inhabitant leaves a lasting vacuity'.[39] This fear was not, however, entirely without national self-interest. Johnson believed that the Highlanders as Americans would cause the crown more trouble abroad than if kept relatively safely at home. It is this theme of emigration that provides one of the most extraordinary of Boswell's descriptions:

> In the evening the company danced as usual. We performed, with much activity, a dance which, I suppose, the emigration from Sky has occasioned. They call it *America*. Each of the couples, after the common *involutions* and *evolutions*, successively whirls round in a circle, till all are in motion; and the dance seems intended to show how emigration catches, till a whole neighbourhood is set afloat.

This formal, aristocratic mimesis of Highland mobility resulted from more disturbing performances:

> Mrs M'Kinnon told me, that last year when a ship sailed from Portree for America, the people on shore were almost distracted when they saw their relations go off; they lay down on the ground, tumbled and tore the grass with their teeth.—This year there was not a tear shed. The people on shore seemed to think that they would soon follow. This indifference is mortal sign for the country.[40]

In his *Journal* Boswell records Dr Johnson's dictum that 'all history, so far as it is not supported by contemporary evidence, is romance'.[41] In dealing with the Highlands, unlike other eighteenth- and nineteenth-century Scottish writers, he maintained complete fidelity. Even a realist as gritty as Smollett succumbs to the commercial and national pressures when he deals with them. For Scott the surrender to commercial temptation was complete. It is hard for us to credit how great was the public excitation caused by his martial Highland fantasies; we still do not realise the ambivalent, insidious national dream he was promulgating.[42]

While this dark dream side is quite manifest in Walter Scott, conventional academic wisdom reiterates that Scott's comonsensical head controls both his sense of history and the form of his fiction. This was not what MacDiarmid thought who believed that Scott's fiction was formulaic propaganda for the national self-betrayal of the Union.[43] Lest this be thought not a literary judgement but merely the brutal intrusion of left-wing nationalism, let us consider a more moderate voice. In 1937 Edwin Muir wrote of Scott:

> His imagination was hampered by practical considerations. His love for Scotland was equally hampered by his adherence to the established order of the Union. This rendered his novels and his patriotism romantic in a bad sense, and made him get out of his own two worlds, the past and present, the cheapest they could give him; that is romantic illusion and worldly advantage.[44]

The temptation to which Scott wholly succumbed was that romantic illusion, hence by definition an ersatz Scotland, was a hugely marketable commodity for a cosmopolitan, middle-brow audience. This audience he both titillated and reassured; the hero's journey through barbaric alien terrain always concluded in the safe return to the paternal arms of commercial rectitude. Temperance and progress were sound coinage. Scott wholly accepted the economic and social beliefs of the Scottish Enlightenment. He gave Robertson's history, 'conjectural history', fictional form.[45] This is not in dispute. What is in dispute is whether this was a distortion of Scottish history by way of a manipulation of fictional means to achieve the ends not of the Scottish people but the pro-Union middle and upper classes to which Scott belonged.[46] G.K. Chesterton's witty remark that the Victorians assimilated history to a three-volume novel with themselves as the happily-ending third volume is a relevant reminder of the dangers of fictionalising history. Essentially Scott's formula, ironic in an alleged historian, was ruthlessly to divide Scottish history into a pre-Union, revolting past and a post-Union condition of anglicised, amiable, prospering consensus. His fictional mode of so doing was to adapt the Gothic novel and the English novel of social comedy, as discerned mainly in Fielding, to these two areas respectively. What then threatened Scotland according to Scott was not the agrarian and proto-industrial turmoil of the late eighteenth and early nineteenth centuries but the reactivation of her fanatical past.

Further, Scott believed implicitly that only the commercial, civilising influence of England could ensure that Scotland would not regress to poverty and anarchy. As Tom Nairn has cogently written:

> For Scott, the purpose of his unmatched evocation of a national past is never to revive it: that is, never to resuscitate it as part of political or social mobilization in the present, by a mythical emphasis upon continuity between (heroic) past and present. On the contrary: his essential point is always that the past really is gone, beyond recall. The heart may regret this, but never the head. As Scott's biographer J.G. Lockhart puts it, quite forcibly, his idea of nationalism was like his idea of witchcraft: 'He delighted in letting his fancy run wild about ghosts and witches and horoscopes . . . . (but) . . . .no man would have been more certain to give juries sound direction in estimating the pretended evidence of supernatural occurrences of any sort; and I believe, in like manner, that had any anti-English faction, civil or religious, sprung up in his own time in Scotland, he would have done more than other living man could have hoped to do, for putting it down'. For all its splendour, his panorama of the Scottish past is valedictory in nature. When he returns to the present—in the persona of his typical prosaic hero-figure—the head is in charge. It speaks the language of Tory Unionism and 'progress': the real interests of contemporary Scotland diverge from those of the auld sang.[47]

The culminating irony in this is that the protesting voices of Scott's English contemporaries, the great Romantic poets, conceived of their England as an increasingly rebarbative, predatory, mechanistic, imperial society. It was to take a later Scotsman, Carlyle, to invert the language of English Romanticism into an imperial rhetoric. In their own age the English Romantics were apprehensive of Scotland as an exporter of the quantifying, callous *apparatchiks* who were to provide the middle management for British Imperialism. Scott neither recognised the political reality of this nor that to fulfil his fictional purpose he had, in a post-Union act of inverted emasculation, to render the great factual and critical energies of the English literary tradition impotent. Thus Edwin Muir writes:

> The eighteenth-century English novel was a criticism of society, manners and life. It set out to amuse, but it had a serious intention; its criticism, however wittily expressed, was sincere, and being sincere it made for more civilized manners and a more sensitive understanding of human life. Scott marks a definite degeneration of that tradition: after him certain qualities are lost to the novel which are not recovered for a long time. The novel becomes the idlest of all forms of literary art, and by a natural consequence the most popular. Instead of providing an intelligent criticism of life, it is content to enunciate moral platitudes, and it does this all the more confidently because such platitudes are certain to be agreeable to the reader. It skims over every aspect of experience that could be obnoxious to the most tender or prudish feelings, and in fact renounces both freedom and responsibility. Scott, it seems to me, was largely instrumental in bringing the novel to that pass; with his enormous prestige he helped to establish the mediocre and the trivial.[48]

We can now perhaps see more clearly why Boswell beat so many retreats from genteel Edinburgh. Unlike Auchinleck, he had no wish to inherit what it represented. Scott is the undisputed possessor of enlightened Edinburgh's vision of Scottish history. Boswell sought the juicily humorous, vital world of Fielding. He sought to escape that prudish gentility which not only stifled him as an individual but restricted his social range as an author. Also unlike Scott, Boswell achieved a creative celebration of the Union and not novels of sterile deviance from both literary tradition and political reality. Beginning this essay with unqualified praise of Boswell's past American scholars, it is fitting to end with similar praise for a new one. In Volume 2 of *The History of Scottish Literature, 1600-1800* there is a brilliant chapter by Gordon Turnbull on 'James Boswell: Biography and the Union' in which he shows how Boswell's great act of biographical homage to Dr Johnson is also an assertion of the political and creative synthesis of Scotland and England. Here, as an example, is Turnbull on Boswell's account of the trip to Iona:

> The Boswellian and Johnsonian texts are here the same. All distinctions of time, place and individual personality, of merely local versions of Christianity, vanish in the sanctity of Iona. Moreover, for Boswell, local versions of nationality, distinctions between Englishman and Scot, are similarly obliterated, cut down by the idea of patriotism on the imaginative plain of Marathon. For Boswell as, he believes, for Scotland, an original magnificence has been lost, but recovery and recuperation follow when great objects have been brought together.[49]

If, of course, the Union had been a merger of the radical and creative energies inherent in both Scottish and English traditions our subsequent literary and moral and political lives would have been less problematic. Even for Boswell, however, while his great biography is a manifestation of a truly creative 'concentric' solution to the problem of his national identity, the Union was a psychic wound which would never heal. It troubled him not least in his dealings with his adopted English father. The *Journal* is replete with barbed repartee on the subject:

> I here began to indulge old Scottish sentiments, and to express a warm regret, that, by our Union with England we were no more;—our independent kingdom was lost.—*Johnson*. 'Sir, never talk of your independency, who could not let your Queen remain twenty years in captivity, and then be put to death, without even a pretence of justice, without your ever attempting to rescue her; and such a Queen too! as every man of any gallantry of spirit would have sacrificed his life for.'— Worthy Mr *James Kerr, Keeper of the Records*. 'Half our nation was bribed by English money.'—*Johnson*. 'Sir, that is no defence: that makes you worse.'—Good

Mr Brown, Keeper of the Advocates Library. 'We had better say nothing about it.' *Boswell.* 'You would have been glad, however, to have had us last war, sir, to fight your battles!'—*Johnson.* 'We should have had you for the same price, though there had been no Union, as we might have had Swiss, or other troops. No, no, I shall agree to a separation. You have only to *go home*.'[50]

Home may have been where the heart was, but for the Scottish aristocratic and professional classes the road led south. As Hazlitt, irritated beyond measure by the profusion and profession of things Scotch, remarked:

So Lord Erskine, after an absence of fifty years, made an appropriate eulogy on the place of his birth, and having traced the feeling of patriotism in himself to its source in that habitual attachment which all wandering tribes have to their places of fixed residence, turned his horse's head towards England—and farewell to sentiment.[51]

At a superficial level Boswell displays all the vices of upper-class Scots on the make. At a creative level he does achieve an extraordinary, indeed, in its time, unique creative synthesis of two literary traditions. Johnson, so hostile to Scots who derivatively mimicked English literature, saw in Boswell not a sycophantic admirer but a fellow great writer.[52] 'This,' he wrote of the *Journal*, 'will be a great treasure to us some years hence.'

Johnson also established a tradition of English criticism of the consequences of the Anglicisation of Scotland. As well as Hazlitt, romantic nationalists of the calibre of Coleridge and Cobbett disliked and feared what this coupling between literary, bureaucratic and commercial elites had brought forth.[53] Cobbett believed that British Imperialism had converted aristocratic Scots into the equivalent of Rome's pro-consuls; the harshest masters of a subjugated people would always cynically be chosen from their own ranks. Cobbett also feared the instrusion into English life of rigid, quantifying, utilitarian Scottish idealogues as the cutting edge of the industrial revolution.

It is ironic that Carlyle should have—exceptionally among Scottish critics— so admired Boswell. In his later stages Carlyle, located in London, is the principal symptom of resurrected, atavistic Scottish energies put to the worshipful service of British Imperialism. In that overwrought, paranoid brain, Calvinism's suspect sense of toil and election wholly degenerate into a messianic sense of personal and national mission. What the last decades of *our* century show is a reawakening, presented as an economic and spiritual renaissance, of what Nathaniel Hawthorne termed the 'one-eyed' monster of English

Imperialism.[54] The present puzzle is whether this nightmare figure is going to shock contemporary Scotland into wakefulness and return her to her search for the freedom and community manifest in her greatest letters and in some of her history. Boswell, with his national anxieties, his intellectual openness, his vitality in life and art, indeed his splendidly eighteenth-century, Mozartian capacity to discuss the deepest questions in the lightest manner, is due for repatriation in such a cause. What is the literary-critical equivalent of killing the fatted calf?

NOTES

1. Quoted in I.S. Ross, *Lord Kames and the Scotland of his Day* (Oxford, 1972), p.258.,
2. Tom Crawford, who has made a singular Scottish contribution to Boswell studies, has a fine appreciation of F.A. Pottle, Frank Brady and the Yale group in his review of Brady's *James Boswell: The Later Years 1769-1795* (N.Y./London, 1984) in *Scottish Literary Journal*, Winter 1986, Supplement No. 25, pp.13-17. The critical tide in Scotland may, however, be on the turn. K.G. Simpson has a chapter on Boswell in *The Protean Scot* (Aberdeen, 1988). With extensive contributions from the members of the relatively new Eighteenth Century Scottish Studies Society a volume of essays, *New Light on Boswell*, edited by Greg Clingham, is forthcoming from Cambridge U.P.
3. *Ibid.*, p.17.
4. *Ibid.*, p.16.
5. *The English Experiment 1785-1789,* ed. I.A. Lustig and F.A. Pottle (London, 1986), p.286.
6. *Ibid.*, pp.64 and 141-142.
7. Quoted in Brady, *James Boswell: The Later Years 1769-1795*, p.222.
8. *Boswell in Holland 1763-1764*, ed. F.A. Pottle (London, 1952). p.49.
9. *Ibid.*, p.254.
10. Muir's thesis (see *Edwin Muir: Uncollected Scottish Criticism*, ed. A. Noble (London/N.Y.), 1982) is that Knox's Calvinist-inspired revolution did extensive, irreparable damage to Scottish creative writing. He saw the subsequent bourgeois, clerical culture of eighteenth-century Edinburgh as arid and prescriptively moralistic. A more positive view of this period is to be found in Richard B. Sher's 'Literature and the Church of Scotland', in *The History of Scottish Literature, Vol. 2 1660-1800*, ed. A. Hook (Aberdeen 1987), pp.259-271.
11. *Boswell on the Grand Tour, Italy, Corsica, and France 1765-1766*, ed. F. Brady (London, 1955), pp.289-290.
12. *Ibid.*, p.294.
13. Quoted in Brady, *James Boswell: The Later Years 1769-1795*, p.146.
14. This aspect of Boswell is finely treated by Michael Ignatieff in his chapter 'Metaphysics and the Market', in *The Needs of Strangers* (London, 1984).
15. *Henry James and Robert Louis Stevenson*, ed. Janet Adam Smith (London, 1948), p.255.
16. *Vol. XXI, Collected Works* (London, 1912), p.203.

17. *The Master of Ballantrae*, ed. Emma Letley (Oxford, 1983), p.5.
18. Boswell's remarks on Scottish language and dictionary thereof are to be found in *Boswell in Holland 1763-1764*, pp.158-163. The project seems inspired by a desire to emulate Johnson and the strong antiquarian impulse present in post-Union Scots.
19. Quoted in F.A. Pottle, *James Boswell, The Earlier Years 1740-1769* (London, 1966), pp.326-327.
20. *Ibid.*, pp.357-358.
21. The complex realistic evolution of Scottish vernacular poetry in the eighteenth century is finely traced by Matthew P. McDiarmid in Vol. I, Introduction to *The Poems of Robert Fergusson* (The Scottish Text Society, 1954).
22. *Robert Burns and the Sentimental Era* (Georgia, 1985). The nature, value and virtue of sentimental literature in eighteenth-century writing is the matter of continuing, complex critical dispute. Janet Todd's *Sensibility, An Introduction* (London, 1986) is first-class. Milan Kundera's remarks on *kitsch* in *The Art of the Novel* (London, 1988), where he bewails the effeminate quenching of the Enlightenment's virile intellectuality, is particularly apposite to Boswell. James Mullan's critical account of sensibility in Scotland, 'The Language and Sentiment', in Vol. 2 of *The History of Scottish Literature*, pp.273-288, is very fine. John Dwyer attempts a defence of these bourgeois aesthetics in *Virtuous Discourse* (Edinburgh, 1988). My own more politically sceptical version of events regarding the Literati's response to Fergusson, Burns and the nature of rural life is 'Versions of Scottish Pastoral: The Literati and the Tradition, 1730-1830', *Order in Space and Society*, ed. T. Markus (Edinburgh 1982).
23. 'Robert Burns', *Edwin Muir: Uncollected Scottish Criticism*, pp.182-183.
24. ' . . . . as I had the honor of drawing my first breath almost in the same Parish with Mr. Boswell, my Pride plumes itself on the connection.' *The Letters of Robert Burns*, ed. Ross Roy (Oxford, 1985), Vol. I, pp.335-336.
25. Introduction, *Boswell on the Grand Tour, Italy, Corsica and France 1765-1766*, p.xi.
26. 'Hawthorne and his Mosses', *Nathaniel Hawthorne's Tales*, ed. James McIntosh (New York, 1987), p.345.
27. *Ibid.*, p.345.
28. 'Was There a Scottish Literature?', *The Athenaeum*, August 1st, 1919. pp.680-681.
29. A.L. Quesne, *Carlyle* (Oxford, 1982) pp.4-7.
30. Gordon Turnbull, 'James Boswell: Biography and the Union', in *The History of Scottish Literature, Vol 2 1660-1800*.
31. *Ibid.*, p.159. Boswell was near-obsessive about his Scottish aristocratic ancestry. He also claimed descent from Robert the Bruce. See *Journal of a Tour to the Hebrides*, ed F.A. Pottle (London, 1963), pp.13-14.
32. 'James Boswell: Biography and the Union', p.159.
33. *Boswell on the Grand Tour, Italy, Corsica and France 1775-1776*, pp.185-186.
34. *Ibid.*, pp.169-170.
35. 'Hawthorne and his Mosses', p.344.
36. *Journal of a Tour to the Hebrides*, pp.106-107.
37. 'The Invention of Tradition: The Highland Tradition of Scotland', *The Invention of Tradition*, ed. E.J. Hobsbawm and T. Ranger (Cambridge, 1983), pp.15-41. A more serious account is given in Tom Nairn, 'The Three Dreams of Scottish Nationalism', *Memoirs of a Modern Scotland* (London, 1970), pp.34-54. I have contributed to this debate in 'McChismo in Retrospect', *The Bulletin of Scottish Politics*, No. 2, Spring, 1981, pp.71-81.

38. 'The Caledonian Antisyzygy and the Gaelic Idea', *Selected Essays,* ed. Duncan Glen (London, 1972), pp.56-74.

39. *A Journey to the Western Islands of Scotland* (Oxford, 1951), p.51.

40. *Journal of a Tour to the Hebrides,* pp.242-243.

41. *Ibid.,* p.392.

42. See my 'Highland History and Narrative Form in Scott and Stevenson', in *Robert Louis Stevenson,* ed. A. Noble (London, 1972), pp.134-187.

43. 'Scott's novels are the great source of the paralyzing ideology of defeatism in Scotland, the spread of which is responsible at once for the acceptance of the Union and the standard of nineteenth-century Scots literature except in the hands of men like the Gaelic poet, William Livingston (1808-1870) who were consciously anti-English—a defeatism as profitable financially to its exponents (Scott, Stevenson, Tweedsmuir, & c.) as it is welcome to English interests.' *Lucky Poet* (London, 1972), p.202.

44. 'Sir Walter Scott (1771-1832)', in *Edwin Muir: Uncollected Scottish Criticism,* p.217.

45. Duncan Forbes's article, 'The Rationalism of Sir Walter Scott', *The Cambridge Journal,* vii (1953-54), pp.20-35 is the seminal discussion of Scott's relationship to Enlightenment historiography. Graham MacMaster's *Scott and Society* (Cambridge, 1981) also illustrates the connection but is more sceptical about its value for Scott's fiction. My own view is that Scott's use of 'conjectural history' was, at best, derivative and in the new conditions of social and political turmoil at the end of the eighteenth century not only redundant but positively harmful to his fictional treatment of history.

46. Scott much suits the modern critical temper of indulging in clever boys pulling out intertextual plums; texts decreasingly relate to reality but obsessively discuss their own natures or incestuously allude to other texts. Coleridge, in his old-fashioned way, simply thought Scott fanciful and not truly imaginative in his extensive, unconscious literary borrowings. See my 'Coleridge, Scottish 'National' Literature and Walter Scott', *Strathclyde Modern Language Studies,* Vol. V (1985), pp.3-20.

47. *The Break-Up of Britain* (London, 1981), p.115.

48. 'Scott and Tradition', *Edwin Muir: Uncollected Scottish Criticism,* p.209.

49. 'James Boswell: Biography of the Union', p.171.

50. *Journal of a Tour to the Hebrides,* pp.23-24.

51. 'On the Scotch Character (A Fragment)', Vol. XII *Collected Works,* ed. Waller and Glover (London, 1904), p.254.

52. Johnson's cursory dismissals of not only James 'Ossian' MacPherson but David Mallet and John Home have, as critical appraisals, stood the test of time.

53. See my 'Coleridge, Scottish 'National' Literature and Walter Scott' and 'Versions of Scottish Pastoral: The Literati and the Tradition, 1730-1830'. See notes 22 and 46.

54. *Mr Hawthorne Goes to England,* ed. James O'Donald Mays (London, 1983).

3

Scottish Education and Literacy, 1600-1800: an International Perspective

R.A. Houston

Many claims have been made about the distinctiveness of Scotland's society in the centuries before the Industrial Revolution. Few fail to include at least a passing mention of her educational system, and for some this is a central element of the 'democratic intellect', a feature of Scottish society which makes it not only different from but better than many others.[1] Possessed from the seventeenth century of a national parish school system and, from the eighteenth century, of thriving universities, this poor and geographically peripheral country managed to create a highly literate population and to generate a distinctive and important contribution to the intellectual ferment of the Enlightenment. Used as a model for schools and universities in a number of countries during the nineteenth and twentieth centuries, the Scottish educational system and its achievements have also served to justify both continuity and change in British education since the early nineteenth century. However, discussion of what made Scotland different has been clouded by rhetoric and nationalist sentiment, hampered by a shortage of hard facts and by implicitly comparative statements about high rates of success which fail to specify similar or different achievements. This essay outlines the educational system in Scotland and the levels of basic literacy achieved, drawing parallels and contrasts with other contemporary European and North American societies.

I

At the core of Scotland's education 'system' were the parish schools established by parliamentary legislation during the seventeenth century. Schools were already extensive before the Reformation, especially in the larger burghs but also in apparently 'remote' rural areas, and the Calvinists were able to build on this established Catholic tradition of educational provision. Documentation on education and literacy during the fifteenth and early sixteenth centuries is notoriously sparse. The church was the main provider of schooling but there were also 'adventure' schools and there were almost certainly more teachers than there were schools since those with ecclesiastical job descriptions such as chaplain could also have been educators. Conceivably, many post-Reformation foundations could have been re-foundations. Furthermore, a 'cultural infrastructure' of printing, book importation and learning was firmly in place by the early decades of the sixteenth century. In short, Scotland participated in the European Renaissance and in the 'educational revolution' of the early modern period.[2]

Protestant reformers of the later sixteenth century were united in their desire to have education widely available, and this wish was expressed by the Scottish Calvinists in their 1560 manifesto, *The Book of Discipline*. Humanists saw education as valuable in itself but the Reformers' principal interest was in preserving and propagating their faith and in generating a supply of able and well-trained officials for church and state positions. While a religious drive existed, secular backing had to wait until the seventeenth century when acts of 1616, 1633, 1646 and 1696 created a framework of parish schools. Landowners or heritors were exhorted and ultimately compelled to pay the capital cost of a school building and provide a salary for the schoolteacher. Similar efforts had been made to establish schools and masters to teach in them at a diocesan level in parts of France and Spain from the 1490s and in certain German principalities during the sixteenth century.[3] Their success had been patchy, as indeed was that of the Scottish campaign in its early years. Yet the seventeenth century did witness an expansion of educational provision in Scotland, especially after the Restoration. Indeed, by c.1700 more than 90% of all parishes in the Lothians, Fife and Angus had settled parish schools and salaried masters (usually also the church precentor or Kirk Session clerk), and a large proportion of these offered not only vernacular instruction but also Latin grammar and literature. This level of achievement may have been equalled in the north-eastern parts of France where the church's full commitment to providing schools had produced one in each parish by 1704.[4] In other areas of Scotland which were less economically developed and less staunchly Calvinist fixed schools may have been thinner on the ground, though it is important not to equate institutions with the totality of educational provision. There may have been other schools and teachers not revealed in a single source and it is important to realise that contemporary documentation under-records the availability of education.

Education was 'subsidised' for those who attended parish schools in two ways. First, because the heritors paid for the school building and a salary for the teacher the *net* cost of education to parents was reduced compared with a wholly fee-paying school. Charitable endowment, which was the core of funding for many of England's grammar schools but which was less important in Scotland, would have performed a similar function. The significance of such subsidies has recently been demonstrated in a comparison of the duchy of Baden in Germany with the Vaucluse area of Provence in France. The former villages possessed considerable communal property, income from which reduced the net cost of schooling to about one tenth of its level in the Vaucluse whose communities were not so favoured.[5] In the current state of research it is not possible to be precise about the actual cost of schooling, and some evidence from the eighteenth and nineteenth centuries suggests that salaries were consistently low and that heritors were able to recoup part of their outlay on schools by other means.[6] This sort of 'subsidy' may have helped to ease the burden of education for many families though probably not to any greater extent than charitable funding of some schools in England. Whether achieved by communal funds, charitable endowment or levies on landowners, similar provisions were found in many areas of Europe. Second, as in all European countries, the church provided funds to help poor but intellectually gifted boys to continue their education beyond what their parents could afford. Kirk Session registers sometimes record payments and loans made for this purpose, though rarely to more than a handful of children at any one time in a given parish. For the majority of pupils, fees were paid by parents to the teacher who kept them.

Many European governments did not turn to national educational campaigns until after the expulsion of the Jesuits in the 1770s.[7] In contrast, Scotland's parish school system was conceived as the first truly national one in early modern Europe. Its creation has been lauded and its achievements extolled. However, the apparent uniqueness, modernity and success of the campaign to generate schools and literacy should not be over-stressed. First, passing legislation was simple enough in seventeenth-century Europe, but enforcing it was another matter, a problem recognised in the 1646 act which required landowners to pay *if they could* and shown in cases of impoverished recalcitrant landowners which have come to light throughout the seventeenth century.[8] Educational provision in the northern and western Highlands and Islands remained poor until well into the nineteenth century, especially if judged by the number of settled schools, though it will no longer do to write off the Highlands as wholly devoid of schooling. In the Highlands the initiatives were probably no more successful than in parts of Louis XIV's France or in sections of the Austrian empire in the later eighteenth century. Given the constraints, achievements by 1700 are noteworthy though it may be that the improving quality of documentation over the seventeenth century exaggerates the impression of improvement.[9] At the same time, the day-to-day running of the schools was charged not so much to secular bodies as to the local Kirks who administered financial aspects, appointments and supervision of curricula and teaching methods. This did not, however, prevent the development of more practical, vocational, vernacular education from the end of the seventeenth century in the larger towns.[10]

Second, most parishes had only one official school and, given the size and population of some Scottish parishes, this was inadequate to house all the 'eligible' children, a problem which was only solved in some communities by the provision of another parish school during the eighteenth century.[11] In practice, therefore, private or 'adventure' schools wholly dependent on fees formed an important supplement to the parish schools. While most adventure schools provided only the most basic instruction, some did offer an extensive curriculum. Fee-paying schools became increasingly important during the eighteenth century, especially in major urban centres, and the newly fashionable training in navigation, mensuration and modern languages was provided principally in them. In that sense, adventure schools were more vocational and 'modern' than the parish schools. In 1818, 31% of Scotland's 'eligibles' were in parochial schools, 43% in adventure schools.[12] It was only in the Highlands and in some of the larger towns that charity schools, run by bodies such as the Edinburgh-based Society in Scotland for Propagating Christian Knowledge (SSPCK), taught significant numbers of children in the eighteenth century. The charity schools turned their attention increasingly to placing adolescent 'graduates' in apprenticeships rather than sending them on to further education. Parish schools formed the core of the educational system, and the example they gave may have helped to create a broader demand for learning satisfied in the charitable and fee-paying institutions which operated alongside the parish school system.[13] However, as in most European countries Scotland's schools were funded from a variety of sources and overlapped in their functions. The system was more codified in Scotland than in some other countries by the end of the seventeenth century but the realities of diverse funding with an emphasis on fees made the practice very similar.

Third, education was not made compulsory by law until 1872. The Kirk made efforts to ensure that all children attended school for a time at least and sometimes tried by threats or inducements to make parents continue to educate their offspring. The Scottish Kirk in the Lowlands was a strong and authoritarian body which intervened in many areas of the everyday life of all members of local communities. It may have been successful in compelling brief elementary education for most children, though there is no clear evidence that it was any more so than, say, the dukedom of Weimar which tried this in 1619 or the Prussian state in 1717. Dutch Calvinists were similarly anxious to protect and propagate their faith through schools but were only able to exert direct ecclesiastical discipline over their own voluntary adherents.[14] The Lutheran church in Scandinavia enjoyed a monolithic control similar to that of Scotland, as did Geneva, though we should not underestimate the Counter-reformation Catholic church's drive for conformity in countries like Spain or France.[15] The campaign for literacy was not confined to Protestant nations. The basic problem was less one of parental 'ignorance' or philistinism than of poverty since 'free' education was not instituted in Scotland until 1889-94. Children were expected to contribute towards the family budget by their labour from as early as eight or nine years old. This meant that boys and girls from ordinary backgrounds would attend school for only two or three years, enough to learn basic literacy but little more. The cost of classroom materials was usually met by parents or by teachers from fees. Girls were almost unknown in Latin grammar classes, and in the countryside these tended to be the preserve of boys from the ranks of lairds, prosperous tenant farmers and well-off local craftsmen and tradesmen, in the towns the middling and upper reaches of merchants, master-craftsmen and professionals.[16]

A brief and discontinuous schooling raises important questions about what was taught and how. Early learning focused principally on rote learning of the religious catechism, psalms and prayers alongside basic instruction in how to read letters, syllables and words. Pupils were taught the skill of deciphering and memorising rather than 'reading' with understanding. Early schooling provided the building blocks for future attainments since it was unlikely that the skills of reading or writing could have been generated spontaneously. Learning outside the school as an apprentice, from peers or as an autodidact could substitute for or, more likely, consolidate and extend early schooling. However, the potential opening up of cultural horizons associated with reading was neither automatic nor immediate, for the emphasis was on transmitting fixed ideas and received wisdom, again a common feature of education all over Europe until the end of the eighteenth century.[17] This was also true of the much-vaunted classical education where pupils learned huge amounts of grammar and literature by heart: more value was placed on correct emulation of classical forms than on creative thought. The quality of instruction was very variable. Almost anyone could set up an adventure school, including widows, brewers and crippled soldiers, while at the parish schools the most important qualification for masters seems to have been their politico-religious reliability rather than their pedagogic ability. The importance of fees must have kept teachers on their toes, and not all adventure schools were run by poorly-qualified teachers lacking in commitment. Literary sources offer prominent examples of gifted and stimulating pedagogues in all types of school. However, we must recognise that stultifying teaching methods and a mixed-ability staff are unlikely to have inculcated any sort of critical understanding into pupils at large.

This problem was not unique to Scotland but afflicted all early modern education despite the efforts of English, Italian and Austrian reformers during the seventeenth and eighteenth centuries to break away from traditional methods.[18] Indeed, and finally, this was not the aim of education anywhere in early modern Europe. Order, stability and conformity were the watchwords of authorities in church and state, obsessed as they were with conserving their power and ideological ascendancy. Scottish children were to be taught the fundamentals of the Protestant religion and beyond that trained for their appropriate station in life. The most obvious example is the 'education for dependence' given to girls. They were taught basic literacy at the same time as boys while also receiving instruction in spinning and housewifery, skills which would prepare them for their allotted role as wives and mothers. More advanced education was rare and usually directed at making middle-class girls into more eligible marriage partners by giving them training in ornamental skills such as French, music or dancing. Parents may have seen things differently but, not surprisingly, realistic ones perceived education as a way to prepare their children to live and work in the existing society. The pinnacle of parental aspiration for most girls was to find places for them in service and to see them make a decent marriage while for their brothers an apprenticeship seems to have been seen as more useful than further education.

II

Young women were banned from attending Europe's universities, of which eighteenth-century Scotland possessed some of the most prestigious. Scotland's universities had participated in the fifteenth-century expansion which characterised most of Europe, and further developments took place in the later sixteenth century, including reforms by Andrew Melville at Glasgow and the foundation of Edinburgh university in 1582. The universities remained small and largely devoted to theology until the later seventeenth century when developments in curricula and teaching methods began to diversify and enliven their intellectual life. Student numbers rose from just over 1,000 to 4,400 between 1700 and 1820 (at a time when population less than doubled) thanks to important changes in teaching methods and curricula. Until 1708 at Edinburgh, 1727 at Glasgow and 1747 at St Andrews students were taken through all the years of their university career by 'regents'. These non-specialist teachers watched over student life and morals, offering instruction by dictating chunks of text to large, passive classes. The pursuit of knowledge and independent thought was restricted by this stress on expounding set texts. The abolition of regenting was followed by the creation of a number of new specialist professorships, notably at Edinburgh, filled by gifted teachers and original thinkers such as William Robertson, Adam Ferguson and Dugald Stewart. The curriculum too began to be modernised from the end of the seventeenth century. Newtonian ideas were incorporated into science teaching and there were developments in theology within an Aristotolean framework. Francis Hutcheson, professor of philosophy at Glasgow, began lecturing in English rather than Latin from 1729. Medicine and the law were famous throughout eighteenth-century Europe for their advanced teaching methods and courses, and were important in changing Scotland's universities from glorified seminaries to much broader institutions which nurtured the distinctive ideas of the Scottish Enlightenment.[19] However, Scotland's universities, like those of England throughout the early modern period, remained principally concerned with turning out clergy until well into the eighteenth century.

Scotland's universities came towards the top of the European league table in the eighteenth century along with those of Germany and Castile in terms of the proportion of 'eligibles' who entered the system. Interpreting sources for university attendance is not entirely straightforward but perhaps 2% of young men matriculated in the early eighteenth century compared with approximately 3% in the early nineteenth, an eighteenth-century increase which (even allowing for the growing numbers of foreign students attending) is unusual in a European context where most universities had seen their attendances peak in the early seventeenth century and fall thereafter until the nineteenth.[20] These figures imply, among other things, that there was an infrastructure of schools teaching Latin, the main entry requirement. What is more, given the variety and high quality of their courses, institutions like Glasgow and Edinburgh were cheap to attend—a fifth or less the cost of Oxford or Cambridge in the early eighteenth century—and drew in an unusually broad social spectrum. Just 27% of students at Oxford and Cambridge were not of the gentry or aristocracy in 1711, compared with 68% of fathers whose sons matriculated at Glasgow in the 1740s who were not from noble or landed backgrounds. By the late 1760s and early 1770s the proportion had risen to 76%. Only the Edinburgh Faculty of Advocates was as élitist as England's universities but only the lesser provincial universities of Germany or Spain and only the glorified grammar schools or *collèges* of France drew in as apparently broad a social spectrum as Scotland's universities.[21] Bursaries helped poor but gifted youths to attend but these were no more common than in the more prestigious universities of Spain, France or Italy, and all over Europe there was a growing volume of complaint from the end of the sixteenth century about the usurpation of such places by the well-off. We should not exaggerate the role of universities in promoting social mobility since most entrants from the lower and middling ranks of society tended to look no further than a modest clerical career and the drop-out rate for the poorer and less well-prepared students was high.

Outside Scotland, the most dynamic university system of the eighteenth century was probably that of Germany. Institutions of higher education there had recovered fairly easily after the holocaust of the Thirty Years' War. Some then began to reform their curricula and teaching methods and there were, unusually in a European context, new foundations at the end of the seventeenth century, notably Halle in Saxony (1694). Their real development took place during the eighteenth century as, under the stimulus of competition from the new *Ritterakademien* (Knights' academies) and of quickening interest from governments and élites, they began to change the subjects they offered and the way they taught.[22] Elsewhere in Europe, individual universities continued to prosper throughout our period—Pavia for medicine, Leiden, Salamanca and Padua for law—and the universities of Castile saw a revival of matriculations in the later eighteenth century. However, few countries could match the range of subjects, the new teaching methods and the brilliant scholarship of Scotland's best universities, and it is no accident that the intellectual developments which made Scotland a leader in the European Enlightenment took place within her universities rather than outside them as happened in France and Italy.[23]

III

The organisation and merits of Scotland's school and university system have been extensively discussed in existing literature. Much less substantial is the body of research on its tangible achievements, especially in terms of basic reading and writing ability. In the middle of the nineteenth century census reports show that the Lowland Scots were appreciably more literate than the English nation as a whole, and it has been argued that the same was true a century or more before this. Scotland has been ranked alongside Sweden, Prussia and colonial New England as one of the most literate countries in the pre-industrial world, or at least that part which used a Latin alphabet.[24] In the absence of questionnaires and 'objective' tests historians can use either direct or indirect measures of literacy in a population. Indirect measures include book production, sales, borrowing and ownership; inferences from the provision of schools; contemporary comments about the level and distribution of literacy among Scotland's people. These sorts of measures are fraught with interpretative difficulties which we shall examine below. More tractable and reliable as a criterion of literacy is the ability to sign one's name in full on a document. From the sixteenth century onwards many surviving Scottish records contain signatures, marks or notarial attestations of illiteracy: bonds, leases, receipts, letters, petitions and court depositions for example. Furthermore, such documents exist in profusion all over Europe and signing ability can therefore be used for international comparison of literacy since the same skill is being measured each time. Above all, the criterion is direct, involving none of the serious problems of inference associated with other measures.[25]

The first point at which a 'snapshot' of literacy is available is at the time of the Scottish Revolution when all adult males were supposed to sign bonds of political and religious association: the National Covenant of 1638 and the Solemn League and Covenant of 1643. Surviving examples from the Lowlands show that roughly three-quarters of adult males were illiterate (unable to sign their names in full on the Covenant) at this time, a figure slightly worse than that for England derived from the Protestation Oath of 1641-2.[26] The following century saw substantial improvements in literacy. Subscriptions to depositions before the central criminal High Court of Justiciary show that men in Lowland Scotland were approximately 35% illiterate in the 1750s, a figure slightly better than England as a whole but identical to that for the four northern counties. It is also close to levels obtaining in north-eastern France and the northern Netherlands, a similarity with areas of widely differing economic, religious and social makeups which is intriguing. Male illiteracy had been halved in just over a century.

For women the successes were more modest. Female illiteracy in the early seventeenth century had probably been far more extensive than male, and even in the mid-eighteenth century 70% of adult females could not sign their names, a level characteristic of much of north-western Europe though superior to large tracts of the rural south where female illiteracy remained almost universal until the nineteenth century. This substantial gap between the achievements of men and women was equalled in the geographical divide between the Lowlands and the interior of the Highlands. Men in the northern and western Highlands and Islands had only achieved levels of literacy by the 1750s similar to those which had prevailed in the Lowlands in the 1640s. In certain areas of the Highlands this was the product of poverty, the limited influence of the Protestant church, absence of schools, the prevalence of the Gaelic language and of oral cultural forms rather than written. The eastern and central Highlands were perhaps closer to the Lowland cultural and educational pattern. Many areas of Europe shared the problem of linguistic or dialect differences—Brittany, the Basque region, Provence, Catalonia, southern Italy and areas of eastern and central Europe. Where the language of law, literature, government and possibly education was different from the local vernacular, literacy tended to develop much more slowly than in 'core' or dominant regions.[27] Gaelic culture was deep and varied (and predominantly oral), but lack of knowledge of English left monoglots isolated from developments such as the Scientific Revolution and the Enlightenment which were slowly enriching Lowland culture.

Differences between the literacy of men and women, Highland and Lowland are very clear in the mid-eighteenth century. Yet Scotland has been likened to places like Sweden or colonial New England in allegedly ironing out the effect of broadly 'environmental' influences on literacy.[28] By the late eighteenth century we are told that all Swedes could read irrespective of wealth, status, gender or place of residence; in contemporary New England signing ability was almost universal among men irrespective of occupation, wealth or residence though female literacy continued to lag behind. We shall turn to reading ability shortly, but we can state that differences between the literacy of social groups and between town and country remained clear in eighteenth-century Scotland as they did over the rest of Europe. Breaking down Lowland society into its most significant groups illustrates the social hierarchy of literacy which followed the distribution of wealth and status. Lairds, nobility and professional men (lawyers, writers, surgeons, teachers and others) were all literate for the period 1700-1770. Craftsmen and tradesmen were roughly 20% illiterate, tenant farmers (a large and heterogeneous group which formed the backbone of Scottish rural society) about 35%, their labourers, cottars and servants 65% illiterate. While less extreme than parts of eastern Europe or southern Castile, these divisions were found to a greater or lesser extent in all European countries. Rural society in southern Spain, parts of Italy and Poland was stratified between a mass of poor peasants and labourers on the one hand and a small percentage of well-off landowners and prosperous tenant farmers on the other. Wider chasms of illiteracy separated the classes than in Scottish, or for that matter English, society. Significant differences also existed between town and countryside. Just 10% of craftsmen and tradesmen living in Edinburgh and Glasgow could not sign their names in the period 1700-70. Those working in lesser urban centres like Dundee, Perth, Stranraer or Stonehaven were 16% illiterate but rural artisans and retailers were 39% illiterate. The urban-rural divide is less pronounced than in, for example, northern Italy but it is the normal pattern all over pre-industrial Europe. Indeed Scotland's eighteenth-century literacy profile squares more neatly with most of north-western Europe than it does with star performers such as New England.

Despite its merits as a universal, standard and direct criterion of literacy, the ability to sign does not command general approval among social and cultural historians. Because reading was taught before (and indeed separately from) writing, it is likely that this skill was more widespread than signing which was in turn more extensive than fluent writing at length. Furthermore, reading gave access to the growing body of vernacular literature and is thus potentially more useful as an indicator of the cultural possibilities opened up by literacy. Indeed, it has recently been argued that possibly by the 1740s and certainly by the 1790s Scotland's people were like those of Sweden in possessing universal reading ability.[29] The Lutheran church in Sweden (and indeed Iceland, Norway and Finland) instituted a campaign during the seventeenth century to educate its flock for religious reasons.The Swedish church of the seventeenth century sought to educate people for religious reasons. A Swedish church law of 1686 made basic reading and religious knowledge a requirement for those who wished to marry, baptise children or give evidence in court. The Swedish campaign was rather different from that of Scotland since Scandinavia had very few fixed schools and most of those were to be found in the dispersed urban settlements. Instead, they began a drive for home learning: clergy and those already literate would teach parents who would then instruct children. The local clergy kept registers of reading ability and knowledge of basic religious precepts among all parishioners, records unique in Europe. These show that by the mid-eighteenth century in Sweden and Iceland reading ability was effectively universal but writing stagnated at low levels until the introduction of school systems in the early nineteenth century.[30] Similar exhortations were made to Scotland's parents by her kirks, but the context of educational development was very different in Scotland from Scandinavia and we should be wary of extrapolating from Swedish and Icelandic examples to argue that Scotland's population had an ability to read which was far higher than levels of literacy as defined by signing.

There is some tentative evidence which suggests that Scotland may have achieved similar successes. Contemporary comments suggest high levels of mass literacy while records of book reading imply an extensive demand for literature, some of it intellectually demanding. These types of source offer indirect measures of literacy, are subject to different interpretations, and widely diverging inferences can be drawn from them. Take the case of generalisations on the basis of remarks made by observers of eighteenth-century society. Daniel Defoe believed that the Scottish people were not only more godly but also better educated than their English counterparts, a sentiment echoed in the early nineteenth century by advocates of educational change in England. It was said that even humble servant girls had copies of Burns' poems, and in his *Rural Recollections* of the late eighteenth and early nineteenth centuries, published in 1829, George Robertson put forward the view that the cottars owned chapbooks while their employers, the tenant farmers, generally had Bibles and other more substantial books among their possessions.[31] These remarks are interesting and implicitly quantitative and comparative but offer us no certain information on literacy. The same can be said of reports made by ministers during the 1790s and collected in the (Old) Statistical Account compiled by Sir John Sinclair. Ministers reported extensive reading amongst their parishioners in a way which suggests that it was commonplace.[32] Yet, since it was the duty of these clergy to ensure that they could read the Bible and the psalm book, it is hardly surprising that they tended to report mass reading ability in their parishes. At the same time, their reports do not offer any clear indication of the quality of reading skills: could people read and understand anything or was it simply a question of rote learning of set texts? The problem of understanding has recently provoked debate among Scandinavian historians who now question the more confident assumptions about the quality of literacy made in the early years of research.[33]

Similar difficulties of inference plague other promising sources. Christopher Smout has recently used records relating to the Cambuslang 'revival' meetings of 1740-2 to argue that, as in Scandinavia, virtually all Scotland's people could read by the mid-eighteenth century whereas signing ability remained socially restricted. The source is a notebook kept by a minister in which he recorded the spiritual biographies of 110 believers, selected on unknown criteria from the thousands who attended the meetings. There is no evidence that these people were typical of all those who were 'born again' let alone of the Scottish population as a whole and we have no direct evidence other than their say so that these people could read.[34] Rather more satisfactory is evidence on book ownership and readership. Lists of those who subscribed in advance of publication to receive a copy are included in some books. These show that there was apparently an extensive demand among artisans for relatively expensive and intellectually demanding literature, a demand which spread further down the social scale than in contemporary England and was possibly helped by steadily rising real wages during the eighteenth century.[35] Printing and publishing were flourishing industries in eighteenth-century Scotland and books were widely available, especially in the Lowland towns. Specialist texts were also imported. Scottish publishing had price advantages over certain other European countries and exported books abroad. Urbanites of the eighteenth century were thoroughly familiar with printed and written ways of transacting business, but how are we to quantify this facility?

One fascinating if rare source is the borrowing register from the library at Innerpeffray near Crieff in Perthshire. This library was set up by a local landowner in the mid-eighteenth century and was available to all those in the area: potentially several thousand people. Its register survives from 1747 until 1962. Between 1747 and 1757, 241 loans are recorded covering 121 men and 9 women. Just under a half of the men were professionals—clergymen, students, teachers, writers and others—while the remainder were mostly craftsmen and tradesmen. Nearly two-thirds of borrowers took out only one book in the eleven-year period and a fifth borrowed two; the maximum number of volumes borrowed was eleven. The reading fare was mainly practical and religious material of a substantial nature. Borrowing and lending may have taken place outside the official borrowing register, people may have read aloud to friends and they may have bought books elsewhere, but rather than indicating extensive book readership this register reinforces the profile of literacy derived from signatures and offers some striking parallels with reading societies in eighteenth-century

Germany. That of Trier in the period 1783-93 had eighty-three members but only two-thirds ever borrowed a book and eight readers accounted for approximately half of the books borrowed.[36] First, reading took place mainly among men and was concentrated in the middling and upper ranks of society; it covered a small percentage of the total population. Second, reading was intensive rather than broad: people tended to peruse one book in detail rather than skimming several works for ideas or novelties. Extensive reading only became the norm in most of Europe during the later eighteenth and nineteenth centuries as is shown in the rapidly growing demand for novels, newspapers and periodicals. Again, the Innerpeffray borrowing register suggests that reading was not particularly widespread in Scottish society and indicates that Scotland was not very unusual in a European context.

IV

A number of general conclusions about the development of European education and literacy can be drawn from this outline of Scottish structures and trends. First, legislation to provide schools is only one way of promoting literacy. In practice the networks of schools across Europe were varied and complex. Funding came from various sources and the provision of schools was crucially complemented by demand for learning. The importance of interactions between institutions and society is further shown in the fortunes of Europe's universities: those like Scotland's which responded to changing demand by reforming teaching methods and curricula flourished, those which did not decayed. Second, the role of Protestantism in promoting literacy is less straightforward than is often assumed. Jesuit schools in Catholic Europe provided excellent education and the example of north-eastern France and of the towns of Spain and northern Italy suggests that Catholic training could be as effective as Protestant in instilling basic literacy. Third, where the language of religion, literature and law was different from that in everyday use, literacy tended to suffer, as it did in parts of the Highlands and in pockets all over continental Europe. Finally, the theory and practice of educational provision was very different from the ostensible purposes of education today. Across Europe the aim was to offer an *appropriate* training and thereby to promote social stability.

There is ample scope for further research into local and regional variations in educational provision. Studies of literacy in local communities could also be conducted though the collection of data from wills, receipts, leases, petitions, bonds and court records would be time-consuming. Some idea of reading tastes and of the quality of reading skills is central to our understanding of the ways in which Scotland's people perceived and utilised intellectual developments though it is clear that we shall have to rely on indirect and largely unquantifiable sources. Levels of attendance at parochial and other schools, the actual cost of education to parents and their attitude towards different types of learning also merit investigation. That this research should be informed by work on other countries has been the principal argument of this essay, for it is only by adopting an internationally comparative approach that the distinctiveness of educational provision and literacy achievements in early modern Scotland can be accurately determined.

NOTES

1. L.J. Saunders, *Scottish democracy, 1815-1840* (Edinburgh, 1950). The issues raised in this chapter are discussed at much greater length in R.A. Houston, *Scottish literacy and the Scottish identity* (Cambridge, 1985) and in *idem, Literacy in early modern Europe: Culture and education, 1500-1800* (London, 1988) which is being published by Longman. For comparisons with contemporary and modern literacy campaigns, see R.A. Houston, 'The literacy campaign in Scotland, 1560-1803', in R.F. Arnove and H.J. Graff (eds.), *National literacy campaigns. Historical and comparative perspectives* (New York, 1987), pp. 49-64. I should like to thank the editor and Callum Brown for their comments on this contribution and also those who attended seminars at the universities of Strathclyde, Liverpool, Dublin, Cork, Belfast and Coleraine where earlier versions were delivered.

2. T.C. Smout, *A history of the Scottish people, 1560-1830* (Glasgow, 1972), pp. 420-50; J. Scotland, *The history of Scottish education*, 2 vols. (London, 1969), vol. 1, pp. 10-21; J.M. Beale, *A history of the burgh and parochial schools of Fife* (Edinburgh, 1983), based on a 1953 Edinburgh Ph.D., remains a model for detailed original research; R. O'Day, *Education and society, 1500-1800* (London, 1982), pp. 217-23; J. Durkan, 'Education in the century of the Reformation', *Innes Review*, 10 (1959), pp. 67-8,76-9,82,84-7; *idem,* 'The cultural background of sixteenth-century Scotland', *Innes Review*, 10 (1959), pp. 382-6. The concept of a major expansion in English education c.1540-1640 was developed by L. Stone, 'The educational revolution in England, 1560-1640', *Past & Present*, 28 (1964), pp. 41-80, though recent work has shown that, like Scotland, the north of England already possessed an extensive school network well before the Reformation: J. H. Moran, 'Literacy and education in northern England, 1350-1550', *Northern History*, 17 (1981), pp. 1-23; H.M. Jewell, ' "The bringing up of children in good learning and manners": a survey of secular educational provision in the north of England, c.1350-1550', *Northern History*, 18 (1982), pp. 1-25.

3. G. Strauss, *Luther's house of learning* (London, 1978); J-P. Dedieu,

' "Christianisation" en nouvelle Castille', *Mélanges de la Casa de Velazquez*, 15 (1979), pp. 261-94; A. Croix, *La Bretagne au 16e et 17e siècle*, 2 vols. (Paris, 1981), vol. 2, pp. 1200-2.

4. D.J. Withrington, 'Lists of schoolmasters teaching Latin, 1690', *Scottish History Society Miscellany*, 10 (1965), pp. 121-30; Houston, *Literacy in early modern Europe*, pp. 32-8, 46.

5. M.J. Maynes, 'The virtues of archaism: the political economy of schooling in Europe, 1750-1850', *Comparative Studies in Society and History*, 21 (1979), pp. 611-25; Houston, *Literacy in early modern Europe*, pp. 53-4. The Scottish system was, in practice, varied and complex. For example, the parish of Kingarth on Bute funded its school in the late seventeenth century from a levy on all householders along with fees: D.J. Withrington, 'Education in the 17th century Highlands', in *The 17th Century in the Highlands* (Inverness Field Club, 1986), pp. 60-9.

6. C. Brown, *A social history of religion in Scotland since 1730* (London, 1987), pp. 90-100 outlines the religious context of educational provision. Salaries were low throughout the eighteenth century and evidence from the nineteenth century shows that schoolmasters derived as much as four-fifths of their incomes from fees. Personal communication from Callum Brown. If this proportion holds for the seventeenth and eighteenth centuries, then Scotland more closely resembled the Vaucluse (and probably England) than it did Baden: Houston, *Literacy in early modern Europe*, pp. 53-4.

7. Houston, *Literacy in early modern Europe*, pp. 40-8.

8. Withrington, 'Education in the Highlands', p. 61.

9. Houston, *Literacy in early modern Europe*, pp. 32-48, 116-29. These source problems have long been recognised and intensive work on a range of documentation has shown a potentially extensive educational network even in remote, often Gaelic-speaking, areas such as Banffshire and Ross. In the presbytery of Dunkeld there are 60 mentions of teachers in 22 parishes between 1661 and 1689. Many recorded teachers were graduates and therefore able to teach Latin and prepare pupils for university: Withrington, 'Education in the Highlands', pp. 62, 64-5. Such enthusiastic revisionism does, however, carry the risk of overstatement and special pleading. For example, is someone designated a 'schoolmaster' in the records active in that role, and if so, who and what precisely is he teaching? Until such questions are answered the traditional picture of Highland society being less well favoured with schools than Lowland must retain some credibility.

10. A. Law, *Education in Edinburgh in the eighteenth century* (London, 1965).

11. Arnove and Graff (eds.), *National literacy campaigns*; Withrington, 'Education in the Highlands', p. 67. In the eighteenth century some larger and more populous parishes did establish more than one official school.

12. T.W. Laqueur, 'The cultural origins of popular literacy in England, 1500-1850', *Oxford Review of Education*, 2 (1976), p. 256.

13. M.T. Clanchy, *From memory to written record. England, 1066-1307* (London, 1979) argues that the extensive use of written record was pioneered by the English crown in the twelfth and thirteenth centuries. The state's insistence on written record eventually persuaded the upper classes to adopt these forms. Clanchy argues that there was nothing intrinsically superior in writing as a way of transacting business and securing title to land, goods and rights but that people had to be *persuaded* to adopt that form. Conceivably the example of the Calvinist church's schools in seventeenth-century Scotland may have encouraged a more general demand for

learning in the population at large, though it is also possible that this interest existed even before the Reformation and would have developed even under a Catholic church during the seventeenth century.

14. Houston, *Literacy in early modern Europe*, pp. 42, 46-47; B.P. Lenman, 'The limits of godly discipline in the early modern period with particular reference to England and Scotland', in K. von Greyerz (ed.), *Religion and society in early modern Europe, 1500-1800* (London, 1984), p. 135; see M. Prestwich (ed.), *International Calvinism, 1541-1715* (Oxford, 1985) for further comparisons.

15. Dedieu, 'Christianisation', pp. 261-94.

16. Houston, *Literacy in early modern Europe*, pp. 48-55, 108-9; *id., Scottish literacy*, pp. 240-43; O'Day, *Education and society*, pp. 226-34, 251-2; Law, *Education in Edinburgh*; my own unpublished research confirms this picture of socially restricted access to Scotland's grammar schools.

17. Houston, *Literacy in early modern Europe*, pp. 12-31; A. Grafton and L. Jardine, *From humanism to the humanities. Education and the liberal arts in the fifteenth and sixteenth-century Europe* (London, 1986). Rote learning was still prevalent until well into the twentieth century.

18. G.M. O'Brien, 'Maria Theresa's attempt to educate an empire', *Paedagogica Historica*, 10 (1970), pp. 542-65; A.K. Liebreich, 'Piarist education in the seventeenth century', *Studi Secenteschi*, 26 (1985), pp. 225-78 and *id.* 27 (1986), pp. 57-89; O'Day, *Education and society*, pp. 179-95.

19. Scotland, *Scottish education*, pp. 134-69; O'Day, *Education and society*, pp. 231-6, 273-9; C. Camic, *Experience and Enlightenment. Socialization for cultural change in eighteenth-century Scotland* (Edinburgh, 1985), pp. 165-84. Not all universities flourished: St Andrews' student numbers stagnated through the eighteenth century.

20. Houston, *Literacy in early modern Europe*, pp. 76-90; Stone, 'Educational revolution'; R.L. Kagan, *Students and society in early modern Spain* (London, 1974); *id.*, 'Universities in Italy, 1500-1700', in D. Julia, J. Revel and R. Chartier (eds.), *Les universités Européennes du XVIe au XVIIIe siècle* (Paris, 1986), pp. 153-86; L.W.B. Brockliss, 'Patterns of attendance at the university of Paris, 1400-1800', *Historical Journal*, 21 (1978), pp. 503-44.

21. V. Morgan, 'Approaches to the history of the English universities in the sixteenth and seventeenth centuries', in G. Klingenstein, H. Lutz and G. Stourzh (eds.), *Bildung, politik und gesellschaft* (Vienna, 1978), pp. 138-64; W.M. Mathew, 'The origins and occupations of Glasgow students, 1740-1839', *Past & Present*, 33 (1966), p. 78; N.T. Phillipson, 'The social structure of the faculty of advocates in Scotland, 1661-1840', in A. Harding (ed.), *Law-making and law-makers in British history* (London, 1980), p. 148. Occupational designations are not an infallible guide to social status and wealth: humble artisans and rich master craftsmen could hide behind the same title. It is still likely that the middling ranks found universities more accessible and appealing in Scotland than in England.

22. R.J.W. Evans, 'German universities after the Thirty Years War', *History of Universities*, 1 (1981), pp. 169-80; C.E. McClelland, *State, society and university in Germany, 1700-1914* (Cambridge, 1980).

23. D. Daiches, P. Jones and J. Jones (eds.), *A hotbed of genius, The Scottish enlightenment, 1730-1790* (Edinburgh, 1986); Kagan, *Students and society in Spain*; *id.*, 'Universities in Italy'. Of course, not all students participated directly in the intellectual ferment of the Scottish Enlightenment. New professorships and new subjects were being established in English universities during the early eighteenth

century but these attracted few students. Common law was taught in the Inns of Court and theology actually became more important at Oxford and Cambridge during the eighteenth century. O'Day, *Education and society*, pp. 269, 271-2.

24.   K.A. Lockridge, 'Literacy in early America, 1650-1800', in H.J. Graff (ed.), *Literacy and social development in the west: a reader* (Cambridge, 1981), p. 188. Scotland's apparent superiority in literacy in the mid-nineteenth century may have been overstated thanks to a concentration on census documents. Data collected by the Privy Council committee on education in 1864 showed that 29% of Scottish pupils failed a writing test compared with 15% of English schoolchildren; figures for reading are 11% and 13%, for arithmetic 33% and 23% respectively: J. Gordon, *The education scheme of the church of Scotland from its origin, 1825 to 1872* (London and Edinburgh, 1873), p. 39.

25.   Houston, *Scottish literacy*, pp. 162-92; *id.*, *Literacy in early modern Europe*, pp. 116-29.

26.   D. Cressy, *Literacy and the social order* (Cambridge, 1980), p. 73; all Scottish figures from Houston, *Scottish literacy*, pp. 33-72; 91; European comparisons from Houston, *Literacy in early modern Europe*, pp. 131-53.

27.   Houston, *Literacy in early modern Europe*, pp. 138-40, 204-13; F.J. Shaw, *The northern and western islands of Scotland: their economy and society in the seventeenth century* (Edinburgh, 1980), p. 144; V.E. Durkacz, *The decline of the celtic languages* (Edinburgh, 1983); C.W.J. Withers, *Gaelic in Scotland, 1698-1981* (Edinburgh, 1984); Withrington, 'Education in the Highlands', pp. 64-5, 67.

28.   K.A. Lockridge, *Literacy in colonial New England* (New York, 1974), pp. 24-5, 60; 'Literacy in early America', pp. 184-7, 195-8; E. Johansson, 'Literacy campaigns in Sweden', in Arnove and Graff (eds.), *National literacy campaigns*, pp. 65-98.

29.   Criteria of literacy are fully discussed in Houston, *Scottish literacy*, pp. 162-92 and in Cressy, *Literacy and the social order*, pp. 42-61; T.C. Smout, 'Born again at Cambuslang: new evidence on popular religion and literacy in eighteenth-century Scotland', *Past & Present*, 97 (1982), pp. 114-27; M. Spufford, *Small books and pleasant histories: Popular fiction and its readership in seventeenth-century England* (London, 1981) discusses what was actually read. An important St Andrews M.Phil. by Charles Lord on the Lauriston Castle chapbook collection of the National Library of Scotland should be available for consultation by the time this volume is published: W.R. MacDonald, 'Scottish seventeenth-century almanacs', *The Bibliotheck*, 4 (1966), pp. 257-322.

30.   V. Skovgaard-Petersen (ed.), *Da menigmand i norden lærte at skrive* (Copenhagen, 1985); M. Jokipii and I. Nummela (eds.), *Ur nordisk kulturhistoria: och folkbildning fore folkskolevasendet* [*Studia Historica Jyväskyläensiä*, 22] (Jyväskylä, 1981); Johansson, 'Literacy campaigns in Sweden', p. 92.

31.   Houston, *Scottish literacy*, pp. 166-7.

32.   J. Sinclair (ed.), *The statistical account of Scotland*, 21 vols. (Edinburgh, 1791-99). Discussion of the ministers' reports is necessarily brief since it is based on unpublished claims made by Mr Withrington at a Scottish Society for the History of Education seminar given by the present writer.

33.   Skovgaard-Petersen (ed.), *Da menigman i norden lærte at skrive*; Jokipii and Nummella (eds.), *Ur nordisk kulturhistoria*.

34.   Smout, 'Born again'.

35.   P. Laslett, 'Scottish weavers, cobblers and miners who bought books in the 1750s', *Local Population Studies*, 3 (1969), pp. 7-15; P. Rogers, 'Book subscription among the Augustans', *Times Literary Supplement*, 15 Dec. 1972, pp. 1539-40, though

subscribers did not necessarily read the books. Information on wages from Christopher Smout.

36.   Houston, *Scottish literacy*, pp. 174-9; R. Engelsing, *Analphabetentum und Lektüre* (Stuttgart, 1973), pp. 56-66, especially p. 63; A. Ward, *Book production, fiction and the German reading public, 1740-1800* (Oxford, 1974).

4

Webster Revisited: A re-examination of the 1755 'census' of Scotland

Rosalind Mitchison

This essay is an attempt to give a new interpretation to the figures gathered, transmuted, but not published, by the Reverend Alexander Webster, minister of the Tolbooth parish, Edinburgh, from 1737 to 1784. Webster had been the organiser of the system of pensions for the dependants of deceased ministers of the Church set up in 1743,[1] and his work in checking the soundness of this pioneer insurance scheme kept him interested in demography for many years afterwards. His 'census' exists in several manuscripts which are not exact copies of one another. One of these, unfortunately not the earliest, was published in 1952 for the Scottish History Society by James Gray Kyd as *Scottish Population Statistics*.[2] In this it can be seen that Webster provided a figure for the population of each parish, divided into Protestants and Roman Catholics, but not separated by sex, added these up to give the total population of Scotland, and divided this again into an estimate of the population of every year of age. An abstract of these figures is also provided under the heading of Age 10, Age 20, i.e. an eleven-year age group followed by ten-year age groups. The figures on which all this was based were provided by parish ministers, usually in the form of the number or approximate number of people on the catechising lists that they had made up, sometimes of figures for the whole parish, but the age structure was based on a previous undated enquiry that he had launched at an unspecified number of selected parishes.

Webster's census was known to various people in the world of politics, and the figures for individual parishes were used by Sir John Sinclair in his *Statistical Account of Scotland* of the 1790s to supplement the figures submitted to him then by parish ministers. It is the basis for frequent statements that the population of Scotland in 1755 stood at approximately one and a quarter million—Webster actually wrote 1,265,380: he should have written 1,269,390. This estimate is probably as accurate as the figure of 1.625 million of the first census in 1801, and should be taken seriously. The same cannot be said of the frequently quoted figure of 1.1 million attached to the year 1707, which is an invention based on misinterpreting earlier writers' guesswork.[3]

The publication in 1981 of E.A. Wrigley and R. Schofield's authoritative and innovative work. *The population history of England, 1541-1871*, makes it desirable to reconsider the currently accepted picture of the structure of the populations of the neighbouring countries. The sources for historical demography in these countries do not enable practitioners to make use of the particular techniques which have achieved so much for England, but English conclusions should be taken as perhaps having implications elsewhere. Wrigley and Schofield show the English demographic system as one of 'low pressure', that is of moderate birth and death rates, and the growth of population as held back till the mid-eighteenth century by relatively late marriage and low nuptiality. Without claiming that all England's neighbours should have similar regimes—and indeed all recent work on France and Ireland has reaffirmed the picture of very considerable differences between these countries and the rest of western Europe[4]—we should note that many aspects of the social system in Scotland were similar to those in England, and be prepared to discuss whether these are not sufficiently powerful for us to expect similarities in the demographic regimes. In particular, the system by which most of the rural population left home before puberty to enter into farm service in the households of other families, and the delay in marriage resulting from the limited number of positions available as tenants, cottars, craftsmen or married servants, might be expected to produce a similar pattern of late and low nuptiality. One might expect population growth to advance even later in Scotland than in England, since in the seventeenth and early eighteenth centuries Scottish economic development, though following the general lines of England, took place much later.

Yet the picture of Scottish population structure in the mid-eighteenth century as set out in M.W. Flinn (ed.), *Scottish population history* in 1977 is of a much more high-pressure system than the English. We are offered a relatively high birth rate, a very high infant mortality rate and a fairly high general death rate. It is generally accepted that Scottish population grew more slowly than English in the eighteenth century, but as yet the contribution of emigration to this feature has not been analysed. The figures for population growth in the two countries as set out by Neil Tranter in the new edition of his *Population and Society* tend to exaggerate the difference, for the writer can use decadal growth rates from Wrigley and Schofield, whereas for Scotland he has only the growth between Webster's census in 1755 and the first census.[5] The resulting contrast is in this form:

	1750s	1760s	1770s	1780s	1790s	1801-11
English population growth rates	.8	.6	1.0	.9	1.1	1.1

	1755-1801	
Scottish population growth rates	.6	1.2

Certainly growth was slower in Scotland. If Webster's total is reliable, the growth between 1755 and 1801 in Scotland was only 62% of that in England.

We can do very little in comparing the experience of the two countries in the century before 1755, for we have little quantifiable evidence to use for Scotland. We know that Scotland contributed on a big scale to the immigration into northern Ireland in the 1680s and 1690s. We also know that the country lost heavily in population in the famine of the 1690s. T.C. Smout estimated the loss at between 5 and 15%, and thought that it had been made up by 1740. Recent work by R.E. Tyson for Aberdeenshire puts the loss there much higher, at 25%, and indicates that it had not been recovered by mid-century.[6] In 1755 Aberdeenshire claimed 9% of Scotland's population, and it may have had an even bigger share in the late seventeenth century. The particularly devastating effect of the famine in the inland areas of Aberdeenshire raises the possibility of equally severe losses in other northern counties, but it is not necessary to extrapolate these figures to the southern lowlands. There is good ground for associating the high levels of death in the north and north-east with a relative failure of the poor law in these areas to force landowners to accept the burden of assessment for the support of people on their estates, a failure largely caused by the generally disorganised and demoralised state of shire government after the revolution of 1689. It is a fact frequently pointed out that Webster's 1755 census places more than half the country's population north of the Tay and the Highland fault: the northern component was only just greater than the southern, but the difference may have been greater in the seventeenth century.

It would be unreasonable to think that the difference in demographic regimes meant that exactly at the Border those in the north could be found breeding and dying more rapidly than those in the south. Indeed one of the few weaknesses in Wrigley and Schofield's work is that the study of individual parishes on which it is based makes relatively little use of the four northern counties of England. Of 404 parishes supplying figures, Northumberland and Cumberland provide five each, Durham another three and Westmorland none. The analysis of marriage in England is based on family reconstitution of only thirteen parishes, none of which lies in the north. The word 'only' here is not meant in any derogatory sense. These parishes so reconstituted had to be suitable for this arduous technique, and the Flinn team decided that no parish in Scotland merited this approach.[7] The only figures advanced for age of marriage in Flinn are those drawn from a short period of exceptionally detailed record-keeping in the Parish Register of Kilmarnock.[8] Yet when the figures from the high-quality English material are compared with those from this one parish, they show considerable resemblance. The figures in revised estimates of Wrigley and Schofield's work show an average age of first marriage for women of 26.6 for marriages in the first half of the eighteenth century, falling to 24.1 in the second half. The Scottish figures from the third quarter of the century show 26.5 as the average for rural brides, but 23.5 for those in the urbanised industrial part of the parish. On the proportions of women never marrying, the evidence for both countries is relatively weak, since this is a point not picked up by the technique of family reconstitution. In a recent revision article for England we are offered the figure of 12% of both sexes not marrying of those born in 1716 and 10% for those born mid-century.[9] The Scottish figures, all for the second half of the century, for women only, show parishes burying elderly women of whom the unmarried amounted to between 7% and 33%.[10] The different bases of the figures and the general scrappiness of the Scottish material make any close comparison on nuptiality impossible.

A further source of evidence for Scotland, which was not used in the Flinn project, has been undertaken by Dr Leneman. This was to collect and assess the retrospective assertions on the levels of births in the parish reports of the *Statistical Account*.[11] These, when set against Webster's parish totals, suggest birth rates in the lower 30s. Of course in many cases these estimates were made from study of the Parish Register, and will suffer from the marked tendency of these Parish Registers to miss events. They will underestimate. Even a well-kept Parish Register will omit children dying unbaptised from the burial register, as well as from the baptism register, so these children will be totally unrecorded. So even when baptisms normally took place at a very young age there will be a percentage of children missing. Leneman's figures from the *Statistical Account* done regionally lie mostly in the lower thirties, and even if these should be increased by one or two, to allow for neonatal deaths, they do not square with the Flinn picture of a high birth rate.

The 'high pressure' system of Flinn gives the following features for a population experiencing level 4 mortality by the Princeton model life tables.

birth rate	41.76
death rate	38.01
expectation of life at birth	26.62
infant mortality rate	238.76[12]

But Flinn also presents the evidence deduced from the Kilmarnock material on the age of marriage and the pattern of birth intervals.[13] The latter varied from 23 months, for the gap between first and second child, to 30 months. Further work on the Kilmarnock register suggests 40 as the average age for a mother at the birth of her last child.[14] Now these figures are not those of a high-pressure system. It would be an interesting computer exercise in simulation for someone to see if it is possible for a stable population with these features of childbearing frequency, and with the high level of elderly women dying unmarried— 33% in Kilmarnock—to have a crude birth rate of nearly 42. At any rate it can be accepted that the evidence in Flinn gives conflicting evidence on population structure.

With this incompatibility in mind it is worth turning again to Webster, as the main piece of general information for mid-eighteenth century Scotland. The uniqueness of Webster's enterprise in his work is not widely enough appreciated. He was attempting to collect figures from every parish in the country, and to assemble them in a way which would provide a national picture. Intellectually he does not compare with the great analysts of population figures of the seventeenth century: Graunt, famous for his work on London; Gregory King's study of Lichfield and his use of the English hearth tax; Edmund Halley's pioneer age distribution for Breslau; all these display more sophisticated understanding of the nature of populations and of the statistical nature of age-specific death rates.[15] But Webster was attempting both directly to collect figures and to use them on a national scale, which means that he was involved in an enterprise greater than those of Graunt or Halley. His problem was that his intellectual equipment was inadequate for his tasks. He made an arithmetical mistake in his addition. He did not understand the difference between a life table, the analysis of the chances of members of a particular birth cohort surviving to particular ages, and of a death table, the probability of dying at a particular age, though he realised that such features were fixed for any particular population. He did not realise that there were survival differences between the sexes, and this fact indicates that he had no acquaintance with the work of either King or Graunt, who both knew this. He failed to see that there must be a smooth progression between the likelihood of dying at one particular age and that at the adjacent ages, in other words that the second differentials of his age figures should change smoothly. Again Gregory King would have put him right. He failed to be consistent in his estimates of the survival chances of child age groups. He did not fully understand that part of the available literature on demography which came his way. In these ways he was inferior to the great men of an earlier age. But he was tackling a big problem at its base, in attempting to use current local information for a national assessment.

Let us assess what he did. At some unknown date he obtained detailed age information from an unknown number of parishes, from, he says, 'a great many Ministers in different parts of the Country'. From these he made out a rough age distribution. In 1755 he wrote to all the parish ministers asking for the return of information about the population of the parish, asking how many there were altogether or how many were of an age to be catechised, and at what age this would start. We have over 200 returns to this enquiry, almost all from North-eastern or Highland parishes, because the enquiry was sustained in that area by the Scottish Society for the Propagation of Christian Knowledge, which was a valuable source of extra schools to parishes.[16] In all the parishes Webster's enquiry had the support of the General Assembly, but in the Highlands it had this further pressure. We have a solitary Lowland return which shows that the enquiry was pursued in the rest of Scotland in the same way and at the same time. Webster also asked the ministers about the number of papists in the parish.

Some answers were for the whole parish, but often in round figures which show that they were merely estimates. Most were of those called catechisable, or 'examinables', and here again round figures prevail, showing that though the ministers had lists of those examinable, they had not bothered to count the names on them but had made an estimate. Webster took the figures, round or accurate, and adjusted them by a figure which he had worked out, to allow for the children under catechisable age. His adjustmenmt quotient was $(30+n)/31$ where n was the age of starting catechising.[17]

The returns do not give a feeling of great accuracy on the part of the ministers but Webster did his best by them. Here are some of them.

Essie.

'The whole number of inhabitants, every Individual included, amounts to five hundred.'

Webster did not have the deep suspicion which should be offered to all round numbers, and accepted this as stated.

Alyth.

'The Number of Inhabitants including every Individual according to a Roll I made last Visitation amounts to very near 2700.'

Webster wrote down 2680.

Balquidder.

(Here the minister had difficulty in keeping tabs on his population. He stated that there were 1269 people over the age of 8 but this) 'is about 100 short of the examination roll because yearlie about the middle of March a great number of children goes to the low country to herding . . .'

Webster put down 1586, and a further 6 papists, which means that he used his formula but did not believe that the number temporarily missing was as great as 100.

Port.

'The number of Examinable Persons is about 1450. The youngest I commonly enlist for Examination is about the age of 8 or 9 years, unless . . . Capacity and Progress in Reading be Extraordinary.'

Webster settled on an age of examination of over 9 and wrote in 1865:

Tillicoultry.

(Here the minister claimed that he had 600 on his list, seceders included.) 'The age at which persons are reckoned examinable is not always the same—but according to the genius of the children, some at 6 or 7 or 8.'

Webster seems to have had a low estimate of the genius level in Tillicoultry, for his adjustment figure assumes over 8 as the age of examination[18]

All this means that Webster's list at the end of parish figures has a spurious exactness though at least for 'papists' the accuracy was real, since the Church of Scotland regularly sent out inquiries about these.

He is sticking to a sound principle, to do the best that can be done with the available information. In this he is to be commended. Unfortunately his best was based on a muddle. This has been explained in Flinn. Webster considered that the existing death tables he knew of, the work as he understood it of Halley for Breslau, and the table based the London bills of mortality, did not suit the population of Scotland in the age-groupings that he had obtained.[19] The mortality of Breslau was too low, that of London too high. But his figure of $(30+n)/31$ is in fact derived from his misinterpretation of Halley. (He did not grasp—and one must sympathise with him—that when Halley wrote 'age 7 current' he meant 'aged 6'.)

Webster added up his parish totals to get a national figure, and then broke this down into age groups. His first groupings were in 10-year sets, except for the youngest which contained eleven years. Then within this larger group he broke the figures down to individual years. Here, as he was constrained by the totals within which he had to work, the adjustments from year to year are not perfectly smooth. The interesting thing is that at this point he is using his own table, not his interpretation of Halley's.

My own view of Webster is that he was an honest muddler. He did not realise that he was using material in contradictory ways. He was confident in the material submitted by the ministers, and here he had some justification, for in the insurance scheme he had devised in 1743 he had had to rely on information from them about death risks, and this scheme is unique in having run successfully for over two centuries. Its success may be mainly due to the fact that improvements in the life expectancy of widows over this period have probably been balanced by improvements for their spouses, but that the scheme worked in the first place was based on a correct estimate of the chances.

The analysis of Webster's population in Flinn was the work of T.B. Hollingsworth, who kindly lent his expertise to the Flinn group. Hollingsworth looked at Webster's ten-year grouping, with its anomalous 11-year start, and claimed that Webster could not seriously have meant to make such divisions. Where Webster had

> 0-10
> 11-20
> 21-30 etc

he must really have meant

> 0-9
> 10-19
> 20-29 etc.

In Hollingsworth's own words, otherwise the divisions set out were 'fantastic'.

Further work has made me doubt whether it really is 'fantastic' to set out irregular age groupings. There are numerous examples of such irregularity in the population returns of ministers to the *Statistical Account*. A quick glance at two counties produces these examples:

Clunie, Perthshire. The population was divided into

> under 6
> 6-30
> 30-40 and then on in ten year groups.

Dailly, Ayrshire. The population was divided into

> 1-10
> 10-20 etc.

In other words, the minister failed to realise that some people were not yet one—a common failing of bad enumerators.

Dalry, Ayrshire, divides the population into examinables, that is those over 6 or 7, and non-examinables.

Newton on Ayr. The population is

> under 7
> 7-14
> 14-20 and then on in ten year groups.[20]

Even the distinguished John Graunt, in his life table, used the ages of 6, 16, 26, 36, etc. It is unwise to assume that ministers in the eighteenth century turned naturally to thinking of numbers by the decimal system.

On the basis of his interpretation Hollingsworth compared the percentages in the age groups under 10, under 20, under 30, under 40, with populations as set out in the Model North section of the Princeton model life tables. He had

> under 10   25.477%
> under 20   44.113
> under 30   60.771
> under 40   74.617

These figures matched fairly well with mortality levels varying from 3.6 to 5, the higher mortality belonging to the younger age groups, with a growth rate of .375% a year, a very reasonable estimate for the early days of accelerated population growth.[21] These mortality levels produce the 'high pressure' picture, giving birth and death rates far above the English for this time.

	Hollingsworth's Scotland in 1755	Wrigley and Schofield's England in 1756
birth rate	41.76	32.82
death rate	38.01	25.90
expectation of life	26.62	37.29

It should be noted that though for the mid-1750s the national figures are very different, in the early 1730s, when England was still experiencing fairly high mortality, its expectation of life was 27.88, not very different from Hollingsworth's Scottish figure. It is possible to see Hollingsworth's picture as conforming to some degree to a stage that England had recently passed through, though if this were the case there is still a big difference in birth rates, the English figure for the early 1730s being only 34.02.[22]

But is it right to assume that Webster meant something different from what he wrote? We need to consider Webster's own statement carefully: 'The Number of Persons stated in a Line with the Age of 10 include all who are 10 years of Age and under'. Even allowing for the fact that the language of demography was not established, Webster seems to be making it quite clear that he meant his odd distribution of years.

Suppose we assume that we should interpret him in his own terms. In that case to get the percentages of those under 10, 20, etc we have to add up the yearly groups and ignore his bigger divisions. The result is to run 7.7% off the first group, 4.1% off the second, 2.6% off the third. We get for the percentage under 10, 23.527 and under 20, 42.323. I have considerable doubt about the capacity of the ministers whom Webster troubled for his first structure to know accurately who, in their flocks, was exactly under 30 and who under 40, so I have not bothered with these older segments. Taking a growth rate of .4% (for which reasons will be given later), I find the figures slide straight into Princeton North mortality level 6, which gives as basic features:

birth rate	34.7
death rate	30.7
expectation of life	31.6
infant mortality rate	222

(Given the nature of Webster's material, it does not seem to me helpful to go to a further place of decimals.) Life expectancy is some 4.5 years more than in Hollingsworth's analysis, part of this improvement being based on a 7% fall in infant mortality. At this level it is very near that derived for England in the early 1740s, 31.7. The birth rate is in accord with the regional figures which Dr Leneman has obtained from the *Statistical Account* for the mid-century, if we accept that most of the ministers are likely to have underestimated births by up to 5% a year. The marked change in infant mortality owes a great deal to the fact that the alteration in the percentage of the under-10s is the most drastic change made to the earlier figures. But the lower death rate and higher expectation of life make more understandable some of the regional figures for these features as established from the *Statistical Account* for the 1790s in Flinn, and the improved national infant mortality estimate of 164.[23] If Hollingsworth's features are maintained, there would have had to be a very drastic fall in mortality levels between 1755 and 1790, whereas with these features the change can be seen as more gradual. The implication is that Scotland had a population structure not very different from that of contemporary England, but still with a higher mortality level. Since the general conclusion of Wrigley and Schofield is that fertility changes were more influential on eighteenth-century population growth than mortality changes, it is interesting to note that the English birth rate remained below the Scottish figure here obtained until the later 1770s.

Acquainted, however, with the building bricks of Webster's figures, and his confused use of them, we should not assert exactness for the new figures. It is wiser to put forward the new conclusions in general terms, and expectation of life of 31, infant mortality in the 220s, a birth rate of approximately 36 and a death rate of approximately 32. There is so much evidence for regional fertility differences in nineteenth-century Scotland[24] that figures deduced from an analysis based on a sample very unlikely to have been regionally balanced, should be taken only with caution. The important feature of the new estimates is that they show that Scotland's population structure was not markedly different from the English.

Demographers have tended to neglect a further set of population figures for mid-eighteenth century Scotland, the so-called Augmentation returns. These are the parish totals collected by the Church in an effort to persuade Parliament in 1750 to increase the stipends of ministers. They present figures for 878 out of the 934 parishes.[25] Correlation of the non-contributory parishes with ministerial vacancies shows that they were collected in 1748-9. Here is a sample drawn from Dunbar presbytery:

Stenton	612
Dunbar	3562
Spott	612
Prestonkirk	1224
Oldhamstocks	612
Cockburnspath	857

and here is part of the presbytery of Strathbogie:

Marnock	2000
Botriphny	1000
Glass	1000
Cairney and Ruthven	2400
Grange	1836

When the figures are related to those for the same parishes in Webster's census, there is a growth of 3.37% between 1748 and 1755, which would mean an annual growth rate of .473. Bearing in mind the growth rate between 1755 and 1801, this seems too high a figure, so I based my analysis of Webster on a figure somewhat lower—.4%. The source of the high growth rate may be some remarkable changes in a few parishes. For instance, if these figures are to be accepted, Lecropt in Dunblane presbytery would have increased from 428 to 577, and Aberlemno in Forfar presbytery from 612 to 943.

The problem, of course, is, are these figures to be accepted? We do not have any description of methodology in their compilation similar to that which partly can be deduced and partly was expressed by Webster. Webster passed some harsh judgments on them. In one of the surviving manuscripts of his work he called these returns 'vague' and 'defective'; he stated that he had not taken account of them in his census. He must, however, have known of them, for he had been monitoring the ministers' scheme since 1743, which had involved keeping in touch with many parishes.

It is clear from the Strathbogie sample that in some parishes ministers had returned very round figures, and for these parishes, 68 in all, we need to exercise caution. But the other parishes eschew such simplifications. Here is part of the presbytery of Forfar:

Kirriemuir	3403
Aberlemno	612

Glamis	1469
Kinnettles	612
Dunnichen	612
Cortachy and Clovell	1143
Rescobie	734

It is a well-known fact that random numbers do not look very random, but even allowing for chance duplications there seem to be too many instances of 612 to carry conviction. Twenty-three parishes are alleged to have this population, and another 23 have 857. Other numbers which crop up with unexpected frequency are:

734	22 instances
979	19 instances
1469	17 instances
1224	14 instances
2449	11 instances

In all, some 338 parishes have numbers which are frequently repeated by other parishes or which differ by only one from a much repeated number. These make up 40% of the parish figures.

It seems likely that these repeated figures were deduced from some round number offered on many occasions by the ministers of the parishes, and given what we know of the information easily available to ministers, it is likely that the original round numbers were of the 'examinables', the estimate of those whom a minister would expect to catechise. Suppose that where 612 appears, it was deduced from an 'examinables' figure of 500. If this were the case, the original figure had been multiplied by 1.224. The same multiplication process would mean that the 14 instances of 1224 came from 1000 examinables, the 23 instances of 857 from 700 examinables, the 19 instances of 979 from 800, the 17 of 1469 from 1200, and so on. In that case 40% of the Augmentation returns were achieved in a way similar to that used by Webster in his census.

The resemblance is closer than that. If we take Webster's adjustment figure for age 8, probably the most popular age for the ministers to start catechising at, since by then many of the children who had gone to school would be able to read, we have a multiplier of 38/31, which is 1.2258. This seems to me remarkably close to the 1.224 adjustment of the Augmentation returns. Is it likely that in the central councils of the Church, where policy decisions were made, there were two amateur demographers with such very similar ideas of the relative size of the juvenile population? Surely what these returns show us is Webster's first attempt at a census.

Why, then, was he so disparaging of them? Perhaps because of the 56 parishes with no return, 6% of the total. Perhaps because he felt that there were too many round figures, either round totals, which were 7.7% of the returns, or of examinables, which together with the round totals would make 48% of the whole. He may have come to realise that ministers might start catechising at different ages. He may also have suffered from an intellectual weakness of early demographers, the belief that population was, except in times of disaster, static: the fact that the total picture the Augmentation returns suggested was one of population growth may have been an argument against accepting them. But what I wish to stress is that if, as I believe, these returns are the work of Webster, then they must be taken seriously, even though not with as much respect as his later work.

Accepting the returns as of value, then we can compare them region-ally with the 1755 picture. The returns are grouped by the ecclesiastical district of the synod, which gives us a reasonable regional structure. Comparing the two sets of figures, we get the following levels of growth in the seven years between the two series:

Lothian and Tweeddale	5.19
Glasgow and Ayr	5.69
Merse and Teviotdale	4.08
Angus and Mearns	6.83
Aberdeen	2.69
Dumfries	8.76
Galloway	4.84
Moray	1.78
Perth and Stirling	3.75
Fife	2.12
Sutherland and Caithness	4.64
Ross	2.66
Argyll	4.43
Glenelg	2.30
Orkney	7.30
Shetland	4. 0

These figures suggest that population growth was already well established in the central valley and, to a lesser degree, the Borders and south-west. It was apparently markedly less established in the north-east, a confirmation of Tyson's conclusions, and it was also slow in the Highlands. If this last point stands up to further investigation, it means that we must see the rapid population growth there, discerned by Flinn as already conspicuous in the 1790s, as starting only late in the century.[26] We have no means, as yet, of knowing whether relaxation of the social and economic restrictions on marriage was the means by which population growth was being stimulated. There is a lot more work to be done before we can make for Scotland even a shadow of the remarkable work which has been done for England by Wrigley and Schofield. But it is the theme of this essay that the sharp contrast which has been drawn between the demographic regimes of the two countries should be abandoned.

NOTES.

1. A. Ian Dunlop, 'Provision for Ministers' Widows in Scotland: Eighteenth Century', *Records of the Scottish Church History Society*, vol. 17 (1971), pp.233-48.
2. J.G. Kyd, *Scottish Population Statistics* (Scottish History Society, Edinburgh, 1952), pp.7-9 for Webster's explanation of his method. See also M.W. Flinn (ed.), *Scottish Population History* (Cambridge 1977), pp.58-64 and 250-7. Flinn's book was the work of a team, and in this team I was responsible for the eighteenth-century part.
3. Flinn (ed.), *Scottish Population History*, p.241.
4. For example, L.A. Clarkson, 'Irish Population Revisited, 1687-1821', in J.M. Goldstrom and L.A. Clarkson (eds.), *Irish Population Economy and Society: Essays in Honour of the Late K.H. Connell* (Oxford, 1981), pp.13-35; S. Daultrey, D. Dickson and C. O'Grada, 'Eighteenth Century Irish Population: New Perspectives from Old Sources', *Journal of Economic History* (1981), pp.601-28; E.A. Wrigley, 'The Fall of Marital Fertility in Nineteenth Century France', Part 1, *European Journal of Population* I (1985), pp.31-60.
5. N. Tranter, *Population and Society* (London, 1985), p.36.
6. Flinn (ed.), *Scottish Population History*, p.181; R.E. Tyson, 'The Population of Aberdeenshire, 1695-1755', *Northern Scotland*, vol. 6 (1985), pp.113-131.
7. The work of examining the old parish registers of Scotland was done with great thoroughness for the Flinn team by Mrs Ailsa Maxwell.
8. Flinn (ed.), *Scottish Population History*, pp.276-9.
9. R. Schofield, 'English Marriage Patterns Revisited', *Journal of Family History* X (1985), pp.2-20.
10. Flinn (ed.), *Scottish Population History*, p.280.
11. These figures are used for regional birth rates in Leah Leneman and Rosalind Mitchison, 'Scottish Illegitimacy Ratios in the Early Modern Period', *Economic History Review*, 2nd series, XL (1987), pp.41-63.
12. Flinn (ed.), *Scottish Population History*, p.259.
13. *Ibid.*, pp.276-9, 287.
14. R. McBryde, 'Nuptiality and Fertility in Eighteenth Century Kilmarnock', unpublished M.A. thesis, Edinburgh University, Department of Economic and Social History (1985), p.55.
15. For Graunt, see Ian Sutherland, 'John Graunt; a Tercentenary Tribute', *Journal of the Royal Statistical Society* series A, vol. 126 (1963); for King, see D.V. Glass, 'Two

Papers on Gregory King,' in D.V. Glass and D.E.C. Eversley (eds.), *Population in History* (London, 1965), pp.159-220: for Halley, see J. Lowthorp, *The Philosophic Transactions and Collections to the End of the Year 1700 Abridged and Dispos'd under General Heads* (London, 1716), vol. 3, p.669. See also Major Greenwood, *Medical Statistics from Graunt to Farr* (Cambridge, 1948).

16. Scottish Record Office (S.R.O.) GD/95/5; GD/95/2/7; CH1/2/98; RH15/201. See also Flinn (ed.), *Scottish Population History*, p.61.

17. D.J. Withrington, 'The SSPCK and Highland Schools in Mid-Eighteenth Century', *Scottish Historical Review* 41 (1962), pp.89-99.

18. S.R.O., RH15/201.

19. A. Webster, 'Explanation of Scheme Third', National Library of Scotland MS 89; A. Webster, *Calculations with the Principles and Data on which they are Instituted* (Edinburgh, 1748).

20. *Statistical Account of Scotland*, new edition, Ian R. Grant and Donald J. Withrington (eds.), vol. XII, p.241; vol. VI, pp.133, 159, 498 (Wakefield, 1977 and 1982).

21. Flinn (ed.), *Scottish Population History*, pp.258-9; A. Coale and P. Demeny, *Regional Model Life Tables* (Princeton, N.J., 1966).

22. For the English figures, see E.A. Wrigley and R. Schofield, *The Population History of England 1541-1871* (London, 1981), pp.528-9.

23. Flinn (ed.), *Scottish Population History*, pp.260-70.

24. M.S. Teitelbaum, *The British Fertility Decline* (Princeton, N.J., 1984).

25. S.R.O., CH/1/5/43. These were drawn to my attention kindly by Dr R. Sher.

26. Flinn (ed.), *Scottish Population History*, p.260.

5

Class and Classification in the Buildings of the late Scottish Enlightenment

Thomas A. Markus

Many are familiar with the hilarious passage from Borges which Foucault quotes in his *The Order of Things* (1970). But it bears periodic repetition. Borges himself was quoting from a 'certain Chinese encyclopaedia' which states that 'animals are divided into the following classes:

> a) belonging to the Emperor
> b) embalmed
> c) tame
> d) sucking pigs
> e) sirens
> f) fabulous
> g) stray dogs
> h) included in the present classification
> i) frenzied
> j) innumerable
> k) drawn with a very fine camelhair brush
> l) *et cetera*
> m) having just broken the water pitcher
> n) that from a long way off look like flies'!

Foucault says that this taxonomy shattered, for him, 'all the familiar landmarks of (his) thought'. Such an upheaval of habitual mental structures is certainly shocking; it is an event compounded of a puzzling paradox, humour or intense emotional experience. It both releases from and threatens the habitual stable order of one's life. This order has a structure—one that modern cognitive psychologists have explored, as for instance G.A. Kelly in his theory of 'personal constructs'.[1] The single most important necessity for such a structure is the establishment of categories and groups—classes—into which objects, phenomena, ideas and people can be fitted, and which are linked to each other in a coherent way. Structure and order depend on classification.

It is through the analysis of language that the creation of classes has been studied in anthropology, linguistics, and the social and natural sciences. Much of the research has been aimed at establishing relationships between classification systems and the social context in which they are created. It has been repeatedly shown that the form and structure of these systems is socially produced by the purposes, power structures, ideas, practices and beliefs—and hence the languages—of the societies which create them. If classification systems play such a key social role one can expect them to be related to buildings—which have equally potent social purposes. I have already considered what is involved in considering buildings as classifying devices.[2] The purpose of this essay is to explore this issue in the context of late Enlightenment, early Industrial Revolution Scotland.

Although it may seen obvious that classification systems—that is the rules about deciding what elements share sufficient features to be put into a class which distinguishes them from another which share different features—are the outcome of the perceptions and values of the classifier, there is considerable and lively debate as to whether all systems are therefore arbitrary and imposed, or whether certain 'natural' structures and classes exist which can be recovered through painstaking empirical observation.[3] Whatever the outcome of this debate, it is clear that the presence of classes is a defining feature of both language and of society. Classification appears to be both a way of constructing the world, so as to *give* it meaning, and a way of *receiving* meaning from it, in turn. It is a dynamic, developing process for an individual as well as a society. It thus clearly has immense potential as both as a creative tool and as an instrument for social control. Not only is there a huge variation in types of classification systems, but also in the balance between their creative and their controlling functions. At times they are capable of generating entirely new insights and discoveries, as in the paradigm shifts of biological taxonomies, notably those derived from the theory of evolution. At other times their rigidity, and the degree of static order they are designed to achieve, border on the pathological.

How important structure and order are to an individual at a given moment in their personal development, or to a society at a given moment in its history, depends on the intensity of new experience or ideas to be coped with, and the degree to which there is a sense of basic security. When there is rapid change, coupled to insecurity, order and structure become more rigid, and classification more dominant as a strategy. Erik Erikson (1950) has described the adolescent search for a purified identity, by which the rich paradoxes and conflicts of the new world which is flooding in are ordered into something bearable.[4] Whilst it is a natural stage, those who remain fixed in it, desperately searching for order in the world for the rest of their lives, become the neurotics. Richard Sennett in his *The Uses of Disorder* (1970) describes how this search for a pure, predictable and orderly environment has become the disease of twentieth-century urban planning.[5]

The late eighteenth and early nineteenth centuries in Scotland are one of those periods of deep fear coupled to immense discovery. On the one hand the rural disruptions, the beginnings of rapid urbanisation, the American and French Revolutions and the Napoleonic wars, the emergence—first on rural sites and then in the towns—of the factory system, and urban disorder gave plenty of cause for fearful and reactionary responses. On the other hand the 'Hotbed of Genius'—the challenge of Hume, Adam Smith, the scientists, the engineering inventions of Watt and others, Scotland's temporary world leadership in medicine and the emergence of the romantic vision—each opened up immense possibilities. A dualism of two kinds is present. First, there is both radical invention and conservative reaction within the intellectual and artistic processes. Their products span a complete spectrum from revolutionary poetry to false pastoralism and from philosophical scepticism to evangelical religious conservatism. Secondly, even the most radical and innovative thought and invention was applied both to challenge and to defend the *status quo*. The theory of the division of labour was applied in industry, and made the factory system possible, but the social relations of masters and labourers were modelled on those of agriculture; Hume's philosophical radicalism was coupled to his celebration of the Glorious Revolution and the Constitution; Robert Owen's visionary communitarian socialism to his entrepreneurial capitalism. The examples can be multiplied from poetry, political philosophy and science.

The effect was to deflect much energy into the maintenance of stable order. And an important part of ordering was classification. In architecture the dualism is equally clear. On the one hand the classicism of the Adam brothers, even its mingling with baronial and castellated features, was a smooth continuation of the tradition of formal order which had its roots in the Renaissance. But something revolutionary *was* taking place—not in the forms which architects used, but in the entirely new functional programmes which had to do with the creation of order in quite new building types. These programmes needed a redefinition of the spatial relationships inside buildings and in new town developments. Fundamental to both the functional and the spatial changes was the creation of new *classes* of function and space— the elements which became organised through design. And these classes had social—that is linguistic—origins.

The use of the word 'class' in the late eighteenth century was limited to educational groupings in schools and Universities based on specialised areas of study, or a group under the tutelage of a particular Professor, or a group of children who have reached an equal ability in literacy, writing or numeracy.[6] The unequal division of resources and status in society, up to about 1780, were described by such words as 'ranks', 'orders' or 'degrees' all of which carried, in their context, connotations of mutual support and interdependency, fixed necessity and 'natural' laws of society. It was only in the late eighteenth and early nineteenth centuries that 'classes' of society came to dominate the political and economic writing, and with it came recognition of conflict of interest. Briggs has explored the emergence of the language of class in social discourse.[7]

To trace the influence of classification on towns and buildings one could examine the ordering drive in utopian planning—Edinburgh New Town, or Robert Owen's *Villages of Unity and Mutual Cooperation* (Figure 1). But individual buildings will show what was going on just as clearly. The new ordering methods are to be found not in the forms, stylistic conventions, of buildings, but in their *functional programmes* and *spatial structures*. In order to look at these, some terms first need to be clarified, in a way which takes as its focus meaning—the meaning of the concrete experience of buildings. This experience has three central components.

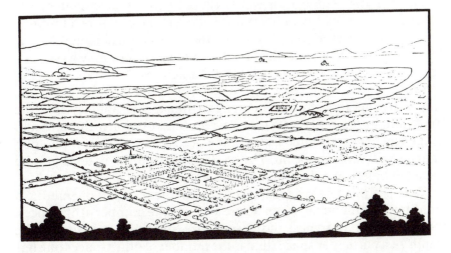

Fig. 1. Robert Owen's *Villages of Unity and Mutual Co-operation*. Source: Robert Owen, *Report to the Committee of the Association for the Relief of the Manufacturing Poor*, London, 1817.

First, and most immediately but not necessarily most durably, we experience what we see: shape, articulation, colours, light-and-shade, formal composition (both in plan and in elevation)—in a word the style of a building. This has meaning which will be recovered in accordance with the formation of the 'reader's' sensibility. Different people will respond differently; and there will be changes over time as the role of imaginative memory changes in the light of associations. The analysis of the meaning of forms involves the study of an interactive process in which both the building and its observer are at the same time formed *by* society and formative agents *of* society. The study of the intersection, at the moment of experience, of these two dual processes is what much of modern art history is about. It is strange that these methods have barely touched architectural history and critique—even though the dominant view of today treats buildings as, primarily, art objects.

The second experience is that of activities. We will see individuals and groups engaged in activities, and we will know what is expected of our participation and what we are expected or allowed to do. If there is no direct evidence of activities, much can be recovered from implicit information such as the location of a space in relationship to others, from its form, and from the nature of its contents in the way of furniture and equipment. It may even carry a verbal label. The language in which whole building functions are described is a shorthand. Such words as 'museum', 'factory' or 'hospital', in a given culture, carry a well-defined package of meanings, as do words for their constituent parts—such as 'catalogue room', 'canteen' or 'ward'. These *de*scriptions are matched by *pre*scriptions, in texts which use the same language, before a building exists. These prescriptive texts are the instructions issued to the designer; today they are called 'briefs'. In the past they may have been letters from a Pope or prince, a town council resolution or an Act of Parliament. All these descriptive and prescriptive texts have the universal property of human language in that the vocabulary used, the length and structure of the text, the degree of elaboration of the parts and its silences are determined by the values and perceptions of the author. Language is never innocent. The analysis of meaning in texts may be rooted in linguistics, discourse analysis or semiotics.

There is a third experience. It starts from the moment of entering a building from the street, when we are aware of the number of entrances. It continues in awareness of the sequence and linkage of spaces, the 'depth' of a particular space (that is the number of other spaces one has to pass through to reach it) and the number of alternative routes to a space (that is whether it lies somewhere along a branching tree, or on a ring). These spatial structures have meanings which are basically to do with control and power and which can be recovered by methods developed by Hillier and Hanson.[8] The spatial experiences relate to function—who does what, with whom, where and controlled by whom; and these, in turn, constitute social structure.

To a significant extent the three experiences—or discourses—of form, function and space are independent of each other. A museum can have any style or spatial structure; neo-classicism does not necessarily entail a specific function or spatial structure; a building with a 'deep', tree-like structure can have any form and serve a wide variety of functions. The questions about meaning have to be asked, in turn, by reference to a field or discourse common to them all, and lying outside them, and then mapped back into a specific building (Figure 2). This field is society itself—its structures and relationships. It is worth asking, in parenthesis, whether, since there is no contingent internal relationship between form, function and space, 'architecture' as a coherent discourse exists. It may turn out to be a field like 'nature', 'family' or 'art'. All these words, whilst depending on well-defined and unambiguous material elements, are mythical in the sense that they are ways of defining reality by the power of abstractions which serve ideological purposes.

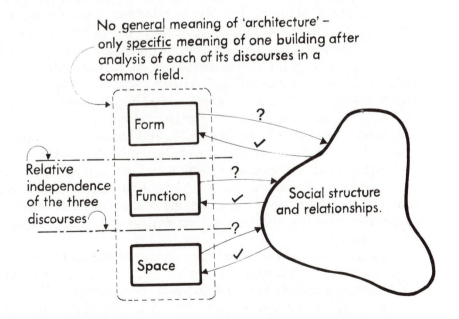

Fig. 2. The social meaning of the three discourses of form, function and space.

Two types of characteristic buildings of this period will be examined to show how classification works as a medium for both creating and understanding buildings. The first type consists of buildings whose purpose is to separate out, contain, make visible and keep under control those who were the most serious threat to an orderly society: the carriers of physical, mental and moral disorder—the sick, the insane and the criminals. These groups were either diffused invisibly throughout the towns and country; or they indescriminately filled various small institutions such as bridewells, town gaols, hospitals, poorhouses and workhouses. With a thoroughness approaching that of the Absolutist Joseph II in Vienna, and of the *ancien régime* Police of Paris, town councils now made a systematic attempt to create large-scale, organised provision for each of these groups.

The earliest example is from Edinburgh where the Infirmary was built in 1738, according to designs by William Adam, father of the four brothers who were later to take Scottish architecture into the international league.

The Infirmary followed an abortive attempt to set up a small surgeons' hospital in the same year. The physicians finally came to terms with the surgeons and agreed to the joint enterprise. Adam adopted a U-shaped plan (Figure 3), the first of a type that survived in British Hospital planning for over a hundred years. Continental practice at this time was more spectacularly formalised, adopting a variety of Greek-cross, radial and pavilion plans, all of which used the church as the focal point. These ideas were rooted in the medieval nave-wards attached to the church (Figure 4) which were further developed in such Renaissance schemes as Filarete's ideal hospital for Sforzinda in the 1460s (Figure 5). Already certain elementary classes were established. The first was gender—male and female—symmetrically balanced on either side of the church. Secondly there were clinical categories, the most important of which was the distinction between infectious and contagious diseases on the one hand, and all the others. Spatially the former were housed in the pest houses and lazarettos outside the city walls, whereas the latter were in institutions integrated into the city fabric.

Adam used the top-floor operating theatre as the central element under the dome, with the proposal that on Sundays it be used as a chapel and on other occasions as an astronomical observatory. By labelling these three classes of function, and thus differentiating them, it was possible to unite them within a single, multi-purpose space. It was also a richly symbolic Scottish Enlightenment project, to combine clinical practice, science and religious worship. If the spatial structure (Figure

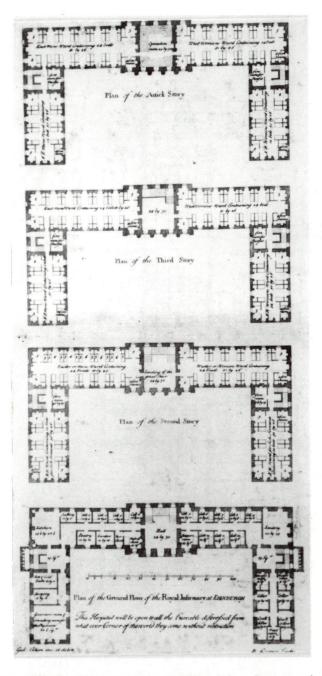

Fig. 3. Infirmary, 1738, floor plans; architect, William Adam. Source and copyright: University of Edinburgh, History of Science and Medicine Unit.

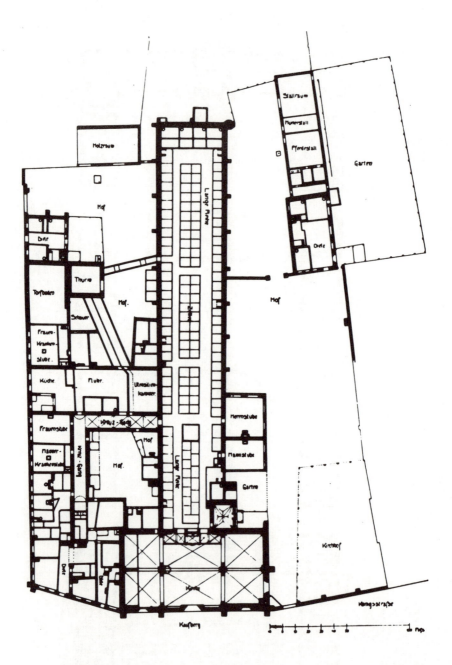

Fig. 4. Hospital of the Holy Spirit, Lübeck, 1287. Source: Dieter Jetter, *Geschichte des Hospitals*, Band 1, *Westdeutschland von den Anfängen bis 1850*, Wiesbaden, 1966, Fig. 11, *after* Gustav Schaumann, *Das Heiligen-Geist-Hospital (in Lübeck), in Bau- und Kunstdenkmaler der Hansestadt Lübeck*, Lübeck, 1906.

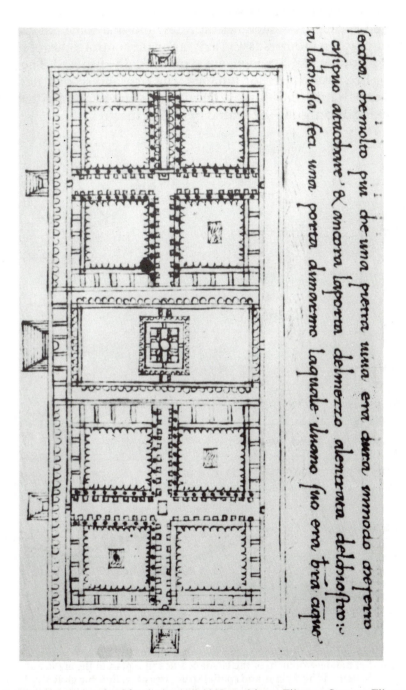

Fig. 5. Hospital design for Sforzinda, 1461-1465; architect, Filarete. Source: Filarete, *Treatise on Architecture*, trans. and with an introduction by John R. Spencer, New Haven and London, 1965, Book XI, folio 82v.

6[a]) is examined, it can be seen that the location of patients' beds occurs at various depths; sometimes on rings; and that some patient spaces control access to others as well as lying on the control routes of staff. The wings, for men and women, are symmetrically disposed. The ground floor had twelve cells for lunatics. The first and second floors were medical wards; the third surgical and lying-in wards, the former opening directly into the central operating theatre.

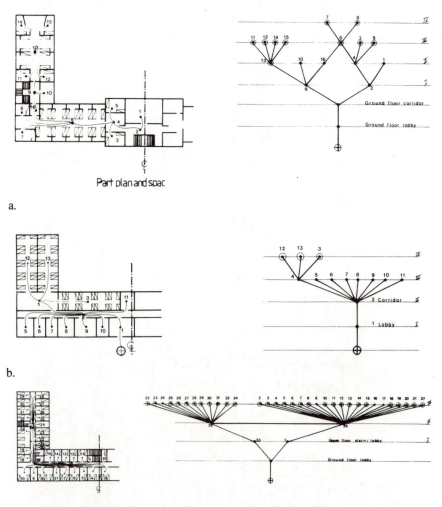

Fig. 6. Spatial development of the U-shaped hospital plan in the eighteenth century. Schematic half plans and spatial structures of: a. Edinburgh Royal Infirmary, 1738; architect, William Adam. b. The London Hospital, 1742; architect, Boulton Mainwaring. c. Manchester Royal Infirmary, with 1793 extension; (architect?).

Adam's U-shaped scheme soon became a model for other British voluntary hospitals; for instance Boulton Mainwaring's London Hospital in 1742 and, a late eighteenth century example, Manchester Infirmary, extended with wings in the 1790s. Although these plan *forms* look similar, significant changes were taking place in spatial structure and function, as the diagrams in Figure 6[b-c] show. The patient areas became concentrated at the deepest level and none lie on any rings; that is to say, there is no communication possible between them other than through points on the shallower rings occupied by the staff. Thus inmate solidarity is prevented by the control of communication. In these plans refinements of medical diagnosis are introduced for classifying the patient areas. Globally, two general categories are created: what Hillier calls the 'inhabitant' domain that is occupied by those who run the institution and invest effort in creating its rules— which is shallow, near the surface—and the 'visitor' domain that is occupied by those who spend periods of days, weeks or months as patients in the hospital—which lie deep within the building. Hillier argues that what *defines* an institution is precisely the inversion of the normal spatial structure of public buildings in which visitors are kept in the outer, shallow layers, and inhabitants control the inner, deep areas.[9]

The buildings for the insane developed in a different direction—on account of the fact that there was continuous ambivalence about the degree to which their disorder was to be treated as a sickness or as a

General View of the Plan of Classification, and of the Distribution of the Classes in the GLASGOW LUNATIC ASYLUM.

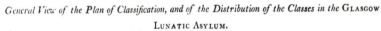

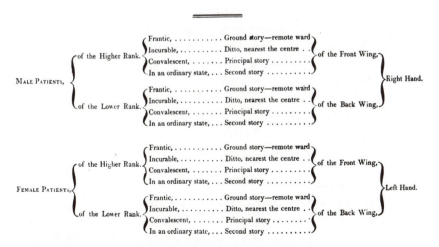

Fig. 7. Glasgow Lunatic Asylum; Stark's hierarchical table of patients and his matching hierarchical locational table. Source: as for Fig. 8a.

criminal, or at least as morally responsible, deviant behaviour. Therefore the regimes had central surveillance as a far more important feature and a startlingly clear statement is made by the Glasgow architect William Stark in his design for Glasgow Lunatic Asylum in 1807.[10]

He set out his brief in a detailed text on the design of such buildings in the form of a diagram (Figure 7). This is hierarchically organised; the asylum, as a total institution, is first divided by economic class—'of the higher rank' and 'of the lower rank'. That meant ability to pay, with special food and even servants, and the pauper patients sent in from the surrounding counties. Next was the classification by gender—male and female. The next division is by medical diagnosis—creating classes of 'frantic', 'incurable', 'convalescent' and 'in an ordinary state'. Each of the resulting sixteen classes was located at specified distances from the centre—according to the principles of isolating the most disturbed and disturbing and of easy surveillance for the remainder.

By careful design of passages to external, high-walled, exercise yards, for 'air and recreation' Stark created face-to-face contact with curative nature without the intervention of others: ' . . .while it may be put completely out of their power to go beyond their own boundary, or to meet with, or even see, any individuals belonging to other classes. In this way each class may be formed into a society inaccessible to all the others, while, by a peculiar distribution of day rooms, galleries, and grounds, the individuals during the whole day will be constantly in view of their keepers, and the superintendent, on his part, will have his eye on both patients and keepers'. The orderly inmates will become less aware of the presence of the keepers, whilst those 'inclined to disorder, will be aware that an unseen eye is constantly following them, and observing their conduct'. So the 'eye' becomes an absolute guarantor of order, classification, segregation and hierarchy—each layer of which is kept under the surveillance of that above.

It is not difficult to argue the case that Stark, and his clients, were using the asylum as a social laboratory and model. It had, in microcosm, all the classificatory and surveillance structures which were found in the cotton mills, in the early monitorial schools and, of course, in the prisons.

The diagrammatic brief, and Stark's whole text, make the resulting design (Figure 8) almost inevitable; a four-armed, Greek-cross plan of three storeys, with a central surveillance zone crowned by a dome. Although this was not in fact a chapel, its cosmic symbolism was deliberate. It was designed ' . . .to avoid a mean and sordid appearance' which could be defended on the grounds of 'ornament'

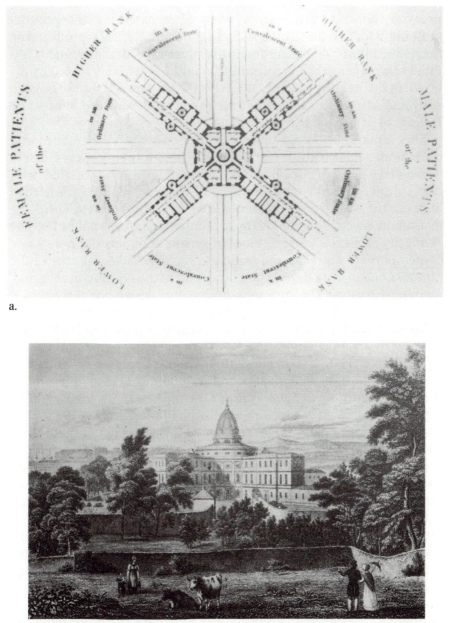

Fig. 8. Glasgow Lunatic Asylum, 1807; architect, William Stark. a. Ground-floor plan.
b. Exterior view by Joseph Swan, 1829. Sources: a. Stark, W., *Remarks on Public
Hospitals for the Cure of Mental Derangement etc.*, Edinburgh, 1807; b. Joseph
Swan, *Select Views of Glasgow and Environs*, Glasgow, 1829.

alone but, in addition, 'it is considered, that a dome of this kind was necessary to unite the different parts of so extensive and peculiar building, which is to last for ages; that a good moral effect is produced on the public mind by the combination of pleasure with utility; and lastly, that as the expense of the institution was chiefly to be defrayed by the board of the wealthy patients, the external appearance should be such as would attract the attention and correspond with the habits and feelings of persons of this description'.

This remarkably lucid statement announces a bold architectural programme. First, to unite segregated classes, a unifying, meta-element is needed—centrally located and psychologically associated with conventional sacred symbolism. Second, elegant camouflage is needed to entice the wealthy—the poor could be forcibly enclosed. Third, the institution was to be long-lasting, a secular sign of eternal order. The similarity of Stark's ideas to those of prison designers did not escape contemporary comment and criticism. Samuel Tuke, founder of the famous Quaker York Retreat and innovator of the non-medical 'moral' regime of treating the insane, admired the design for the views it afforded patients of the country, but complained that Stark did not sufficiently distinguish between the principles of prison and asylums.[11]

It was in prisons that the unseen eye, in total and perpetual control, most completely dominated design. And it was here that classification and segregation of both classes and individuals became the central theme of reform from John Howard onwards. After a long series of experiments to achieve security and surveillance, Jeremy Bentham's Panopticon idea burst on the scene in 1791. It was a circular building, with a central inspection tower, in which every inmate would be continuously surveyed by the governor from the centre; the lighting was so arranged that he could see all but be seen by none (Figure 9). This was the simple, obsessive idea. Bentham refined this proposal to the last detail—sanitation in the cells, one-way listening tubes for each cell to the centre, so that every whisper could be heard; productive labour; religious services conducted from the surveillance tower; segregation of individual prisoners and of classes of prisoners during outdoor exercise. Although Bentham's idea was to have long and deep influence in nineteenth-century Britain, Europe and America, only one actual building was designed on his principles, and that was Edinburgh's 1791 new Bridewell whose architect was Robert Adam. Markus (1982) gives a detailed history of this project.[12]

Adam had already prepared two rather grandiose, conventional designs in that year, before he heard of and met Bentham and enthusiastically embraced the Panopticon—in a *semi*-circular version.

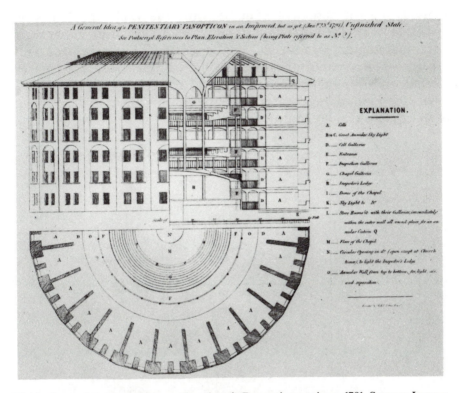

Fig. 9. Second version of Jeremy Bentham's Panopticon prison, 1791. Source: Jeremy Bentham, *Panopticon; Postscript*, London, 1791.

He prepared three new designs in rapid succession, the last of which added day rooms on the inside of the outer cells (Figure 10). This outraged Bentham—for, at a stroke, the chief principle of continuous surveillance was destroyed. At night the prisoners would be out of sight! A furious correspondence ensured, but it was too late; that is how the prison was finally built.

A key aspect of the design is based on classification. It was necessary, with minimum staff, to survey the prisoners in their segregated cells and also when in their classified outdoor exercise yards. Two central surveillance towers were therefore needed. On plan it looks as if the second one, for surveillance of the outdoor exercise yards, is deep in the inner recesses of the building. Formally it is, but spatially far from it. For by the simple device of an underground tunnel which links the two towers—along which the governor would pass backwards and forwards, invisible both to the prisoners and to his own assistants—the inner tower was brought to the surface of the spatial structure. (To demonstrate this, in Figure 11, an earlier version of Adam's Panopticon is used, since a basement plan, showing the vital tunnel link, is available.) Thus the inhabitant, outer zone and the visitor, inner zone were maintained, against all the topological odds. Bridges and tunnels—that is spatial tubes that can connect otherwise distant spaces directly and bring them into topological adjacency—are a standard device for maintaining control without disrupting the classificatory set of spaces in which the controlled are located.

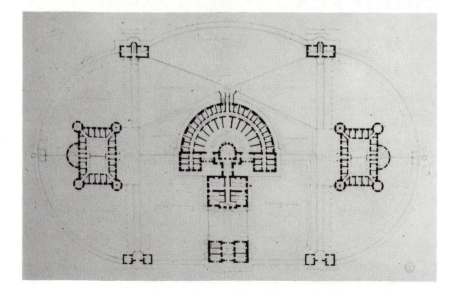

Fig. 10. Edinburgh Bridewell, 1791; architect, Robert Adam. Fifth design, ground-floor plan. Source: Sir John Soane's Museum, London. Copyright: Royal Commission on the Ancient and Historical Monuments of Scotland, Edinburgh.

Many questions arise about the Bridewell. Why was Scotland's capital the *only* place in the whole world where an unadulterated (apart from the day rooms) Panopticon was built? What mixture of utilitarianism, law, and philanthropy made it possible? Why was the image that strange Adam-esque mixture of classicism with baronial, ecclesiastical and military overtones? Why was it prominently located on Calton Hill—on an eminence of the new, classical order, facing the castle on the high point of the old order? Cockburn in fact bitterly complained of the use of the site for this, and later for one of the new monitorial schools founded on the principles of Joseph Lancaster, '. . .where it was the fashion to stow away everything that was too abominable to be tolerated elsewhere'.[13]

For the second type to be considered, a single example—Glasgow

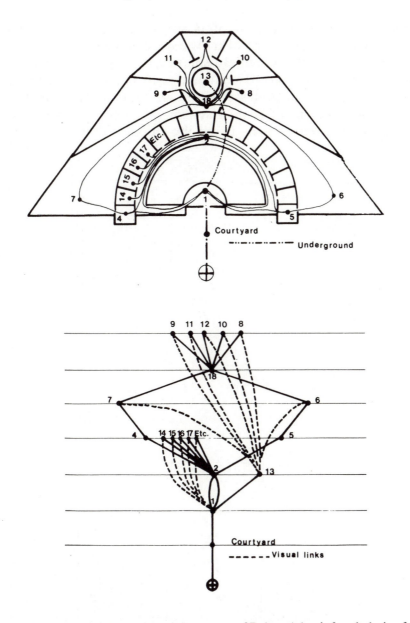

Fig. 11. Schematic plan and spatial structure of Robert Adam's fourth design for the
Edinburgh Bridewell.

University's Hunterian Museum—will be examined (it has been
analysed in detail by Markus, 1985).[14] Unlike these institutions for
classification of people, this is chosen to represent the type of building
dedicated to the classification of ideas and objects; the type comprises
libraries, museums and art galleries. Of course any building which by

definition is designed to house a set of classified objects, becomes a kind of spatial catalogue of some part of knowledge. Leibniz's library for the Duke of Brunswick at Wolfenbüttel displays in the spatial organisation of the books Leibniz's post-Baconian classification system for all knowledge. The individual classes and their sequence were the two defining characteristics of such a system, whether inscribed in a catalogue or arranged, as here, under the elliptical dome of Korb's

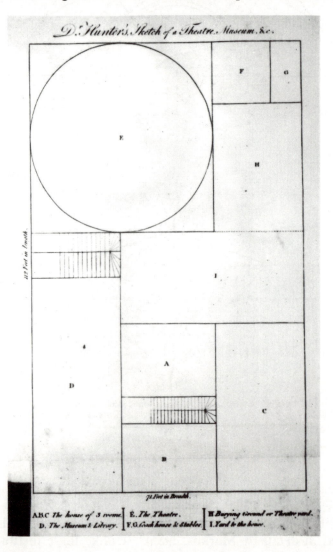

Fig. 12. William Hunter's sketch plan for his proposed school of anatomy, house, library and museum, 1763. Published posthumously, 1784. Source: *Two Introductory Lectures etc.*, London, 1784.

Baroque building. The present-day British Library does the same. But William Hunter's Museum, small as it was, aimed for a more universal representation of man and nature.

William Hunter was London's leading surgeon and 'man-midwife' in the latter half of the eighteenth century. As far back as 1763 he petitioned the Government to grant him the land and funds for building a house, anatomy school and museum. The prototype he designed (although it

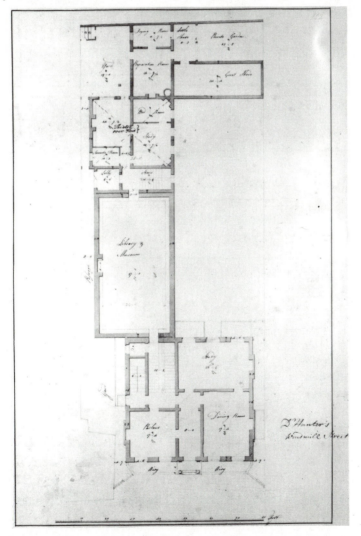

Fig. 13. William Hunter's Great Windmill Street Museum and Anatomy School, London, 1768; architect, Robert Mylne. Source: drawing in possession of Glasgow University. Copyright: Wellcome Institute for the History of Medicine, London.

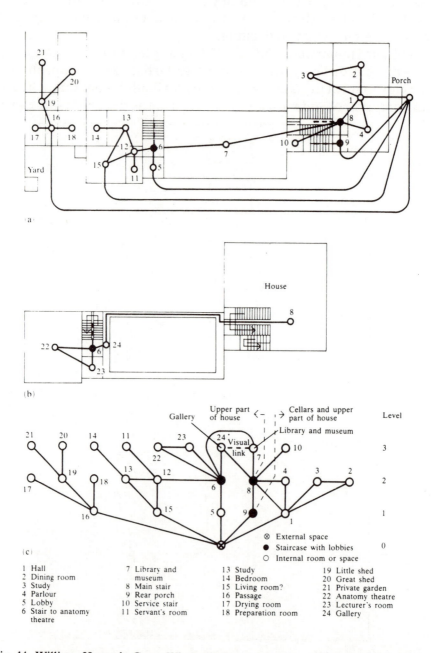

Fig. 14. William Hunter's Great Windmill Street Museum and Anatomy School.
a. Schematic ground-floor plan; b. Ditto, (reconstructed) first-floor plan;
c. Spatial structure. Source: Markus, T.A., 'Buildings as Classifying Devices',
Environment and Planning B, 1987, Vol. 14.

was only posthumously published in 1784) established several important principles (Figure 12). It had the house on the public, street, front. It seems to have had a separate, side, entrance for the students attending the anatomy school. The two were linked by a library and museum. The arrangement suggested a certain order between control, teaching/demonstrating and stored knowledge. When the proposal failed to attract official support, Hunter bought a house in Great Windmill Street and in 1768 employed the Scottish architect Robert Mylne to redesign it and add the museum, library and anatomy school (Figure 13). A spatial map (Figure 14) shows these three key spaces all to be at level 3. The museum was arranged, according to contemporary observers, to show the continuous gradation of nature, from stones, shells, various classes of plants and animals, to the higher-order mammals and finally to man. This represented the unbroken 'Great Chain of Being' which Pope had celebrated and which was the end-point of a long philosophical tradition starting with Plato's principle of plenitude (according to which all possible kinds of things exist) and Aristotle's principles of continuity and gradation. It was essential, for these principles to remain intact, to deny the existence of extinct species—hence the long debate about the Irish Elk. Calculi—stone-like formations in the human being—formed a class of special interest as there was doubt about where in the Chain they should be located, and hence where, in the museum, they should be located. For a long time it was believed that they were actually organic growths of the body, and not inert stones.

But Hunter went far beyond merely classifying the natural world and human organs. All human learning and art became part of his system. Thus books, paintings, sculptures, antiquities, coins and medals all formed important and interconnected collections. Each was classified according to the most modern scholarship in its field and all were connected by Hunter's philosophical system. That system determined the spatial organisation of the whole building, down to the arrangement of individual cases and library shelves.

When Hunter died in 1783 and left his collections, and a capital sum for building a museum to house them, to Glasgow University, a long legal battle ensued. Eventually, by 1799, it was resolved and Robert Mylne submitted the first design for the new museum (Figure 15[a]). Although in plan form it departed greatly from its Great Windmill Street predecessor, its spatial structure (Figure 15[b]) shows startling similarities. The three classes of function (library, museum and anatomy teaching) assume the identical position, at level 3, and are similarly interconnected. Eventually, after a number of designs by Glas-

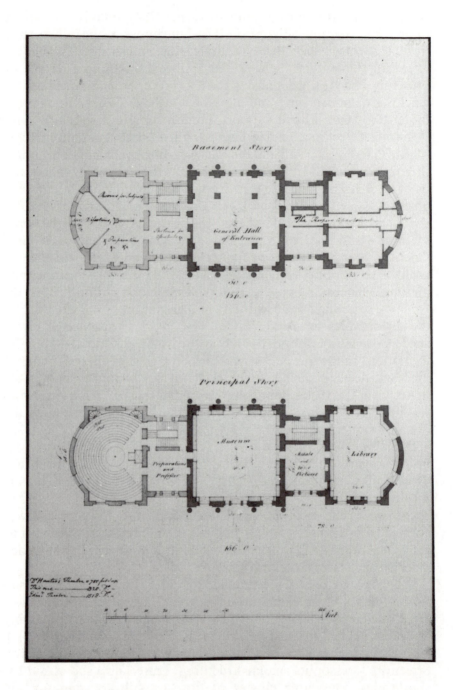

Fig. 15a. Proposal for the Hunterian Museum, Glasgow, 1799; architect, Robert Mylne.
Source: drawing in possession of Glasgow University.

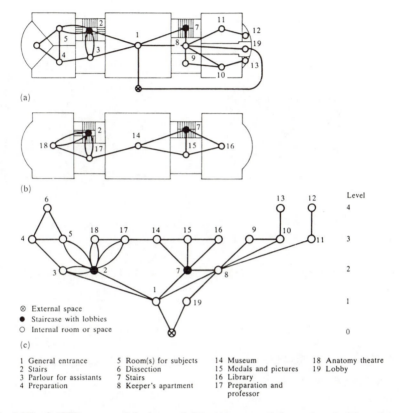

(a)

(b)

6   13   12   Level
                4

4   5   18   17   14   15   16   9   10   11   3

3   2   7   8   2

1   19   1

⊗ External space
● Staircase with lobbies
○ Internal room or space

(c)

1 General entrance	5 Room(s) for subjects	14 Museum	18 Anatomy theatre
2 Stairs	6 Dissection	15 Medals and pictures	19 Lobby
3 Parlour for assistants	7 Stairs	16 Library	
4 Preparation	8 Keeper's apartment	17 Preparation and	
		professor	

Fig. 15b. Mylne's 1799 proposed design: a. Schematic ground-floor plan; b. Ditto, first-floor plan; c. Spatial structure. Source: Markus, T.A., 'Buildings as Classifying Devices', *Environment and Planning B*, 1987, Vol. 14.

gow's leading classical architect David Hamilton were rejected, it was Stark who was commissioned. His design departed not only formally, but spatially, from the earlier schemes. Planned on three floors (Figure 16), with a dominant central dome, it incorporated (perhaps *invented*) a key museum feature—the 'triple fork'. If the spatial structure (Figure 17) is examined closely it will be seen that on both the ground floor and on the first the space under the central, cosmic, dome (marked by a dotted ring) is the root of this fork. The three spaces represented by the three prongs projecting to the next deepest spatial layer contain, in the central prong, a new function. The two lateral prongs contain the same function as that of the space at the root. The root and the two lateral prongs show some aspect of the visible world, leading to, and embracing, at the centre, some aspect of the invisible world. On the ground floor this progression is from specimens of natural science, displayed in their outer forms, to anatomy—the invisible, underlying structure of bodies.

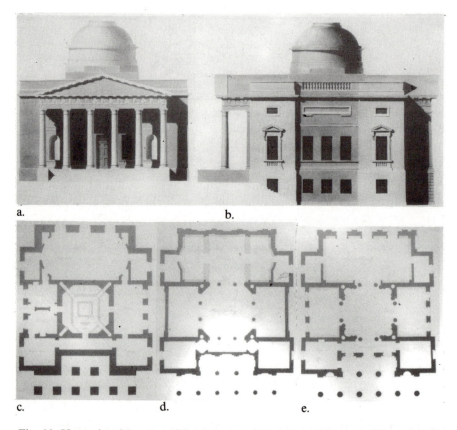

Fig. 16. Hunterian Museum, Glasgow, executed design, 1803-4; architect, William Stark. a. Front elevation; b. Side elevation; c. Basement plan; d. Ground-floor plan; e. First-floor plan. Source and copyright: Scottish Record Office, Keeper of the Records, Edinburgh.

On the first floor it is from the world of the visible forms in paintings to the invisible world of knowledge, contained in books. There is some evidence that this spatial device became a widely-adopted one in the nineteenth century, though not sufficient confirmatory research has yet been carried out.

Hunter became the first Professor of Anatomy at the Royal Academy of Arts within a week of its foundation in 1768. He taught its painters and sculptors that the outward forms of the face and the human body were expressive of emotion, and created empathy in the viewer but only if the artist understood the underlying structures and principles. Otherwise their representations would be dead. So an understanding of the skeleton and the shape of the muscles and organs was essential; but he also maintained that, apart from such anatomical knowledge, the

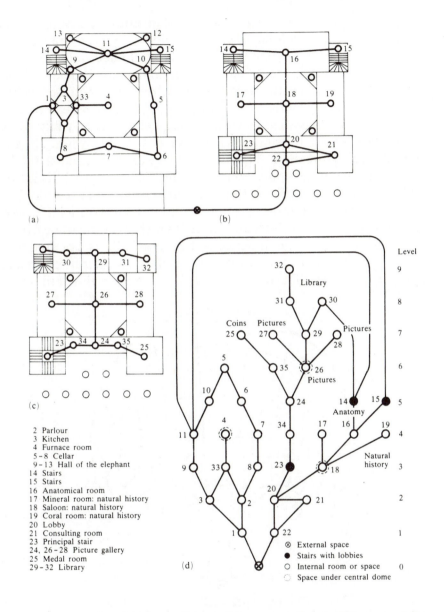

Fig. 17. Stark's executed design: a. Schematic basement plan; b. Ditto, ground-floor plan; c. Ditto, first-floor plan; d. Spatial structure. Source: Markus, T.A., 'Buildings as Classifying Devices', *Environment and Planning B*, 1987, Vol. 14.

painters also had to understand the function of organs, through the study of physiology. Thus form, spatial location and function were, for Hunter, the three vital discourses of meaning which comprehensively explained the body.

The search for underlying rules, laws and structures, which would explain empirical evidence and experience, was a particularly characteristic Enlightenment project. It continued into the early nineteenth century in such fields as phrenology in whose amazingly powerful development and wide influence Edinburgh and the brothers Combe played a vital role.[15] Not surprisingly the idea of the formation of the brain into classified zones of feelings, abilities and traits, whose shape determined thought and behaviour, would eventually find architectural expression. The French utopian industrialist Godin, follower of the philosopher Fourier, in the 1840s designed his factory settlement at Guise in Picardy on the principle that his workers would only be happy if the buildings followed phrenological principles. Since three zones of light, fresh air and space (Figure 18) lay near the front of the brain, the scheme was designed with these as its basis. The analytical sciences of the nineteenth century, particularly in their three greatest exponents of Marx, Darwin and Freud, followed in this tradition of

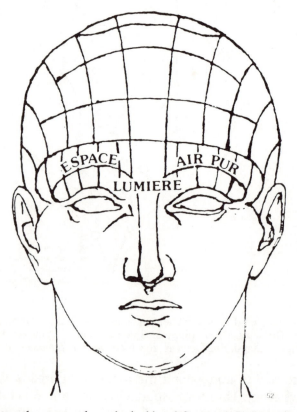

Fig. 18. Nineteenth-century phrenological head. Source: J.-B. André Godin, *Solutions Sociales*, 1871.

discovering and classifying the below-the-surface structures of history, nature and experience. Such an enterprise is still at a very early stage in our studies of buildings and their meaning.

One could also follow the development of the idea of class and classification in the early nineteenth-century monitorial schools—those great 'moral steam engines'—in which children were classified according to closely observed and continuously-tested skills in

Fig. 19. Plate V, first version, of Piranesi's *Carceri*. Source: G.B. Piranesi, *Carceri*, 1745 (?).

performance. Under the all-seeing eye of the master or mistress, with assistant teachers, head monitors and monitors, a clockwork hierarchy was created which became the utilitarian embodiment of Rousseau's and Locke's philosophies. The 'natural' child, and the child free from 'innate ideas' inspired Robert Owen, Bell, Lancaster, Wilderspin and the great Scottish educationist, David Stow. His Glasgow Normal School (the first real training college in the world) still displays his motto, from the Book of Proverbs: 'Train a child in the way he should go and when he is old he will not depart from it'. That training consisted essentially of forming in the child's mind ideas of classes of moral attitudes, objects, social roles and skills which would provide a stable, unalterable framework for the remainder of his or her life.

The rigidity of these classes affected architecture, as all other processes by which society produces and reproduces itself. Not least in the classification processes in buildings was the use of the *classical* language of form. Piranesi in his great *Carceri* series of etchings was exploring a fundamental paradox of architecture (Figure 19). Here there are vast subterranean spaces—ambiguous, paradoxical and dynamic—with staircases leading to nowhere, impossible perspectives and unfinished vaults. All the categories of classical form and space are dissolved. Above the ground, glimpses can be caught of a light, orderly, upper world, obeying all the rules of the Academies and Schools. It seems likely that Piranesi saw that world of reason, light and order as the real prison, which sits on the hidden, dark, disorganised, unclassified, creative forces of human nature and society. The title of the etchings is merely evocative—they have nothing to do with prisons as such. But they have everything to do with the paradox that architecture is committed to creating order by devising structures, rules and classifications. Insofar as it succeeds, it is alienating and imprisoning. His was a search for a deeper, structure-less order such as would have been totally unimaginable to the thinkers or architects of the Enlightenment. Perhaps it remains unimaginable.

NOTES

1. G.A. Kelly, *The Psychology of Personal Constructs* (New York, 1955).
2. Thomas A. Markus, 'Buildings as Classifying Devices', *Environment and Planning B: Planning and Design*, vol. 14 (1987), pp.467-484.
3. A good review of this debate can be found in R.F. Ellen and D. Reason (eds.), *Classifications in their Social Context* (London, 1979).
4. Erik H. Erikson, *Childhood and Society* (New York, 1950).

5. Richard S. Sennett, *The Uses of Disorder: Personal Indentity and City Life* (London, 1970).

6. D. Hamilton, 'Notes on the Origin of the Educational Terms "Class" and "Classroom" ', *Discussion Note, Department of Education, University of Glasgow* (1980); *idem*, The Language of Class Revisited: *Outline Research Proposal, Department of Education, University of Glasgow*, (1982).

7. A. Briggs, 'The Language of "Class" in Early Nineteenth Century England', in R.S. Neale (ed.), *History and Class: Essential Readings in Theory and Interpretation* (Oxford, 1983).

8. W.R.G. Hillier and J. Hanson, *The Social Logic of Space* (Cambridge, 1984).

9. *Ibid.*

10. W. Stark, *Remarks on Public Hospitals for the cure of Mental Derangement etc.* (Edinburgh, 1807).

11. S. Tuke, 'Practical Hints on the Construction and Economy of Pauper Lunatic Asylums', in J.B. Watson and J.P. Pritchett, *Plans, Elevations and Description of the Pauper Lunatic Asylum lately erected at Wakefield for the West Riding of Yorkshire etc.* (York, 1819).

12. Thomas A. Markus (ed.), *Order in Space and Society: Architectural Form and its Context in the Scottish Enlightenment* (Edinburgh, 1982), Ch.1.

13. Henry Cockburn, *Memorials of His Time* (Edinburgh, 1856).

14. Thomas A. Markus, 'Domes of Enlightenment: Two Scottish University Museums', *Art History*, 8, no. 2 (1985), pp.158-177.

15. Roger Cooter, *The Cultural Meaning of Popular Science: Phrenology and the Organisation of Consent in Nineteenth Century Britain* (Cambridge, 1984).

6

The Emergence of the New Elite in the Western Highlands and Islands, 1800-60

T.M. Devine

Over the last decade or so a number of studies have considerably enlarged historical understanding of Highland society in the eighteenth and nineteenth centuries.[1] The majority of these works, however, tend to concentrate on the experience of the ordinary people, the crofters and cottars who suffered the trauma of eviction, emigration and destitution as powerful economic and social forces gripped the western Highlands and islands in the century after 1750. Less attention has been devoted to the landed class.[2] Indeed, when the landowners are brought on to the historical stage, they often simply feature as yet another influence affecting the lives of the majority of the population. Studies which focus directly on the experience of the Highland landed class *per se* are still relatively few in number and, as a result, many profound gaps exist in our knowledge. These deficiencies, however, do not always inhibit the tendency to draw general conclusions about landlord behaviour on the basis of a few examples which may or may not be representative.[3]

The primary purpose of the present essay is to try to partly fill one of these gaps through an analysis of the great transfer of estates which occurred in the western Highlands in the half-century after c.1800. The nature of the development will be probed as well as the motivation of those who sought to purchase Highland land. The focus of the study is almost entirely confined to the mainland parishes of the west coast from Morvern to Cape Wrath and includes all the Inner and Outer Hebrides. The empirical basis of the investigation can be found in the Appendix (pp 136-142) where details are presented of 44 individuals who purchased estates in this region in the period 1800 to 1860. The list does not pretend to be an exhaustive one. On the whole it is likely to be fuller for the large properties than for the small estates. Nevertheless, it offers a reasonable sample of information on the increasing numbers of those from a diversity of wealthy social backgrounds who for one reason or another acquired Highland property in this period.

1

At the end of his long career as Engineer with the Scottish Fishery Board, in the course of which he travelled widely in the Highlands, Joseph Mitchell noted the transformation which had occurred in the pattern of landownership in the region since the 1820s: 'I have seen nearly two-thirds of the estates in the Highlands in my time change proprietors'.[4] Mitchell did not exaggerate. Between 1820 and 1860 several Highland landed families who had held extensive territorial possessions for many generations disappeared from the scene. The empire of the Macdonalds of Clanranald, which included Arisaig and Moidart on the western mainland, the smaller islands of Eigg, Canna and Muck and South Uist in the Outer Hebrides, vanished after a series of sales between 1813 and 1838 which eventually realised more than £214,000.[5] Walter Campbell of Islay, at one time the owner of the entire island, was forced into bankruptcy in 1848 and his estate sold off in 1853.[6] The extensive lands of the Mackenzie Earls of Seaforth, in Lewis and Kintail and Glensheil on the mainland, had almost all passed out of their possession by 1844.[7] Knoydart, the last possession of the Macdonnels of Glengarry, was sold in the 1850s. The McNeills of Barra, Macleod of Harris, Macdonald of Bornish and Macdonald of Boisdale, all lost their hereditary estates in the three decades after the end of the Napoleonic Wars.

But this was not all. Even those landed families who managed to survive were forced into massive sales of parts of their patrimony to maintain solvency. The estates of Lord Reay, in the western Sutherland parishes of Tongue, Durness and Edderachillis, were bought up by the Duke of Sutherland in 1829.[8] Lord Macdonald lost North Uist but managed to preserve some of his family's possessions in Skye while the Macleods of Macleod were forced to sell Glenelg on the mainland and the unentailed portions of their property in Skye in order to escape a greater calamity.[9] Even such grandees as the Dukes of Argyll and the Dukes of Gordon did not remain immune. The Duke of Gordon surrendered territory in Badenoch and Lochaber in the 1830s and the Argyll family put up for sale much of their possessions in Mull and all of their lands in Morvern which had been annexed from the Macleans of Duart in the later seventeenth century.[10] The Morvern estate was exposed to sale in 1819, and from then until 1838 every single property in the parish changed hands.[11]

By the 1850s the pattern of landownership in the western Highlands and islands had been transformed. All of the Outer Hebrides had been sold out of the hands of the hereditary proprietors. Large parts of Skye, most of Mull and all of Raasay, Ulva, Islay, Lismore, Rum and Eigg in the Inner Hebrides had new owners. Only Coll, Tiree, parts of Skye and Jura remained under the control of their traditional proprietors. On the western mainland, Knoydart, Moidart, Glengarry, Glensheil, Arisaig, Kintail and Morvern were all dominated by the new elite. Only in parts of Wester Ross, especially in Gairloch, Applecross and Lochbroom parishes, in the county of Sutherland and in Ardnamurchan, was there substantial continuity of ownership from earlier days. It was a social revolution quite staggering in its scale. From John Bateman's survey of British landownership, published in 1882, it is possible to calculate that at that date new purchasers had acquired 1,139,717 acres or about 60 per cent of the territory occupied by larger estates in the west Highland and Hebridean region outside the county of Sutherland.[12] Even this figure does not do full justice to the real significance of the new landed families. Bateman excluded estates of less than 3000 acres from his survey and it is known that many new purchasers tended to acquire properties below this size in islands such as Mull and mainland parishes such as Morvern. A calculation based on his survey, therefore, is likely to exaggerate the continuity of ownership of large estates among hereditary proprietors. The entire acreage owned by new purchasers was in reality probably closer to at least 70 per cent of the mainland and insular parishes of western Argyll, Inverness and Ross by the last quarter of the nineteenth century.

Precise final figures may be in some doubt but there can be little uncertainty about the significance of what had happened. The scale of land transfer in this region was exceptional both when compared to patterns in the eighteenth-century Highlands and to the general structure of the land market elsewhere in Britain in the nineteenth century. Before 1800 the Highland land market was relatively stagnant.[13] Most of the limited activity which took place merely served to tighten the control of the greater proprietors and as a result there had been a slow but nonetheless perceptible fall in the total number of owners. In the county of Argyll, for instance, the number of proprietors dwindled from two hundred, in the middle decades of the eighteenth century, to 156 by the end of it.[14] Most Highland land in this period was also bought by Highlanders; the acquisition of estates by Lowland or English interests was unusual. For instance, the purchase of the Islay estate and part of Jura by the Campbell family of Glasgow merchants in 1723 was somewhat exceptional.[15] Throughout the seventeenth and eighteenth centuries the greatest transfers had occurred through political rather than directly economic means, for instance as a result of the Argyll annexation of the Duart lands in Mull, Morvern, Tiree and Coll in the 1670s.

The pattern after 1800, and especially after 1810, differed from earlier times in two crucial respects. First, and most obviously, there was an unprecedented acceleration in the rate of estate sales. The information contained in the Appendix reveals that at least 55 properties, several of them of very substantial acreage, were exposed to sale in the region of study. The final figure is likely to be significantly higher than this since a number of estates, such as Arisaig, Glenelg, Glengarry, Lochalsh on the mainland, and insular properties in Mull and Morvern, changed hands more than once during this period. For instance, in 1851 there were 21 separate estates in Mull. All, with the exception of five, had been acquired by purchase, between 1810 and 1850. Several had been sold once and some twice or more during this time.[16] The year of transfer of 48 of the 55 properties mentioned in the Appendix is known. Only three were sold between 1810 and 1819 but thereafter the rate of transfer quickened. Six were sold between 1820-29; 15, 1830-39; 8, 1840-49; and a further 8, 1850-59. In the eighteenth century the west Highland land market was very sluggish; by the third decade of the nineteenth century it had become exceptionally active.

Secondly, there was an equally stark contrast in the type of purchaser over the two periods. In the nineteenth century only eight sales involved resident Highland purchases, by far the most significant of these being the acquisition of the Reay lands by the Duke of Sutherland. But all of these transfers took place between 1813 and 1829. No significant example has been discovered of a Highland resident with hereditary connections with the region buying Highland estates after that period. From 1830 all of the properties listed in the Appendix were acquired by Lowland or English interests, though several had family ties with the Highlands. Indeed, not less than fourteen of the 45 purchasers in the sample were either English landowners, merchants or financiers. Several, such as the Bristol merchant James Baillie, who bought Glenelg, Glensheil and Letterfinlay, the London merchant, Edward Ellice, owner of Glenquoich and Glengarry, and James Morrison of Morrison, Dillon and Co. of London, who acquired Islay on the insolvency of Walter Campbell, soon became among the largest landowners in the Western Highlands and islands. After c.1820, therefore, there was a radical change not only in the pace of land transfers but in the social composition of the purchasers of property. The traditional pattern of steady territorial aggrandisement by the greater Highland landowners was replaced by the large-scale and rapid penetration of a new breed of proprietors from outside the region. Of the

29 non-Highland purchasers whose occupational and social background can be identified, at least in general terms, thirteen were landowners from the Lowlands or England, ten were merchants and financiers, four were professionals (three lawyers and a university professor) and two were industrialists.[17]

This inward movement temporarily reversed the trend towards concentration of ownership which had been occurring in the seventeenth and eighteenth centuries. The spate of land sales which ended the territorial dominion of the Macdonalds of Clanranald between 1813 and 1838 resulted in the emergence of nine separate owners in an area where there had previously been one.[18] Similarly, while the Lewis estate of the Mackenzies of Seaforth was preserved intact when it passed to James Matheson, the family's mainland property in Kintail and Lochalsh was subdivided among several newcomers.[19] One purchaser bought the Islay estate but quickly began to carve other properties out of it.[20] The Duke of Argyll's lands in Morvern were put up for sale in 1819 in five separate lots and were further subdivided thereafter. In the later seventeenth century there were six proprietors in Mull; by the middle decades of the nineteenth century, the number had risen to 21.[21] Yet, this argument ought not to be pushed too far. The penetration of newcomers did not necessarily accelerate the fragmentation of ownership in all areas. Sutherland remained broadly inviolate, with only James Matheson's purchases of Achany and Gruids in that county marginally affecting the pattern of ownership. But the hegemony of the Dukes of Sutherland was secure and their territorial predominance was further consolidated by the acquisition of the Reay lands on the west coast. More important, however, was the emergence of new proprietors, who in certain districts sought to build up great landed possessions which eventually equalled or surpassed even those of some of the ducal grandees whose estates had long dominated the Highland region. The most remarkable examples of this pattern were the two Matheson baronets, Sir James, the owner of Lewis and parts of Sutherland and Wester Ross, and Sir Alexander, proprietor of a number of estates in Ross-shire.[22]

The main significance, however, of these massive land sales in the western Highlands only becomes apparent when they are compared with the condition of the land market elsewhere in Britain at this time. There seem to have been two key differences. First, there was a contrast in the phasing of sales.[23] In both the western Highlands and in other regions the volume of transfers was relatively high in the 1820s. This was to be expected as deflationary pressures after the Napoleonic Wars forced those with high fixed charges based on wartime values to unload some parts of their property on to the market. But in England the velocity of land sales diminished in the 1830s and the years from then until the 1850s have been described as 'a twenty year period of relative stagnation'.[24] The main factor seems to have been the abatement of the flood of forced sales in the immediate postwar period. It was a quite different pattern in the western Highlands. If the data in the Appendix provide a reasonably accurate guide to the chronology of land purchase in the region, there were more than twice as many transfers between 1830 and 1839 as in the period 1820 to 1829. Furthermore, at least eight major properties changed hands between 1840 and 1849 and a further eight in the following decade. There are obvious indications here that the land market in the western Highlands was subject to a series of specific regional influences which maintained sales at a high level despite the reduction in transfer which was occurring in many other areas of Britain.

Second, the scale of land sales, especially of large, self-contained estates, the ebbing of the control of hereditary owners in some parts of the region and their entire disappearance in others, together with the unprecedented influx of new proprietors, had few parallels anywhere else in Britain. Indeed, recent research on the structure of the British landed class and the purchase of landed estates by successful businessmen has tended to show that the number of *arrivistes* who achieved landed status actually declined after c.1820.[25] It is asserted that even in the most rapidly growing economy in the world, few of the mercantile and manufacturing classes had the resources to acquire large landed estates, especially when the availability of marketable properties was effectively limited by the legal devices of trusts, entail and strict settlement and by the stability of the agrarian economy. One calculation, for instance, suggests that in Britain as a whole only 15 of the 200 landlords owning 25,000 acres or more in the mid-nineteenth century were first-generation merchants or industrialists.[26] Interestingly, three of the five greatest such 'new' landowners, Sir Alexander Matheson, James Morrison and James Baird, were west Highland proprietors. The key problem for the historian, therefore, is not simply to offer a general explanation for the pattern of land sales in this region but to explore the particular and specific reasons why the volume of transfers and the numerical increase in the number of 'new' proprietors was much greater than most other areas of Britain in this period. Current interpretations suggest that it was only from the 1870s and 1880s, with the onset of the Agricultural Depression, followed soon afterwards by the introduction of death duties in 1894, that the selling off of lands by hereditary owners became common elsewhere in the country.[27] In the western Highlands and islands, however, the power and position of most of the old elite had already been eclipsed by the middle decades of the nineteenth century. It was the era after the Napoleonic Wars which saw the end of the old order there and it is the particular factors which became significant in that period which now require close examination.

2

The first point to stress is that from the 1820s large areas of land in the western Highlands became available for sale to an unprecedented extent. Most of these sales were forced, in the sense that hereditary owners parted with territory because of the threat or the reality of financial disaster. One student of the British landed class has noted that it was only when a family's predicament became 'exceedingly grave' that landowners would 'sell parts of the family lands big enough to mutilate or destroy the historic character of the estate'.[28] This apparently happened over and over again in the region of study from the second decade of the nineteenth century. Lord Reay sold off his ancestral estates in the west of Sutherland and retired to a villa in Ealing.[29] Walter Campbell's bankruptcy forced the sale of his Islay estate.[30] A similar fate overtook McNeill of Barra. Macdonald of Clanranald had had to sell a number of his hereditary properties in Moidart, Arisaig and the Small Isles between 1813 and 1827 until he was left with only the family lands in South Uist and Benbecula. But the financial pressures were still inexorable, and despite the fact that Clanranald opposed the 'alienation of . . . my last remaining possession' and showed considerable tenacity in trying to retain it, his Hebridean estate was eventually put on the market by his trustees in 1839.[31] So too were the lands of the Mackenzie Earls of Seaforth in Lewis and the western mainland and the family patrimony of the Macdonnels of Glengarry, the last remnant of which, Knoydart, was brought to market in the 1850s.[32]

But even those who managed to retain some possessions and maintain at least a dynastic presence in the region were also often forced to put up some of their lands for sale in order to escape even greater disaster. From the early years of the nineteenth century, Macleod of Macleod (notably with the sale of Glenelg in 1810), Lord Macdonald, the Duke of Argyll (who sold Morvern and parts of Mull from 1819) and the Duke of Gordon released much territory on to the market.[33] Clearly it was not simply the smaller proprietors and those with medium-sized estates who experienced great and recurrent difficulty in these years. It was also ducal grandees such as Argyll and Gordon who were forced into substantial sales in order to ensure their solvency in the long term. Only the immensely rich Sutherland family had apparently the resources in the western Highlands at this time not only to maintain their hereditary position but to add to it substantially in 1829 through the acquisiton of the Reay estates.[34]

It is important to emphasise that forced sales on the scale which has been described were quite unusual in the British context at this time. The volume of land transfers did rise elsewhere in the 1820s but there is little evidence in any other region of Britain of a financial catastrophe on the scale which overwhelmed the west Highland landed elite in the postwar period.[35] As one writer has put it: 'The demise of Highland families in the period 1770-1850 suggests that, in financial terms, the class committed suicide'.[36] In nineteenth-century Britain, however, it was exceptional for great landed families to be completely ruined or to be so severely embarrassed by the accumulation of debt as to be stripped of most of their inheritance. Such examples as the Duke of Buckingham, who went bankrupt in 1848, the Duke of Newcastle, the Earl of Winchilsea and Lord de Marley, who were all before bankruptcy courts in 1870, were untypical.[37] Acute financial difficulty, on the other hand, was the characteristic pattern in the western Highlands and islands in the 1820s, 1830s and 1840s and actual insolvency was far from being an unusual occurrence.

The reasons why the Highland elite should be so much more vulnerable to financial embarrassment than their peers in other regions of Britain are still imperfectly understood. There is a tendency in some writing on the subject to imply that they were responsible for their own sorry plight because their indulgence in wasteful expenditure led to dissipation of the windfall gains of the good years of the Napoleonic Wars in conspicuous consumption (often in the southern capitals) and careless mismanagement of their inheritance.[38] Considerable emphasis is also placed on the extraordinary debt burdens which many proprietors accumulated in this era. On this count, it is argued, they merit criticism for not having the good sense to live within their means. Sir James Riddell of Ardnamurchan had debts of £50,000 in 1848.[39] Lord Macdonald owed over £140,000.[40] Clanranald's debts totalled over £100,000 as early as 1812 and the Earl of Seaforth was burdened with debt in 1815 to the extent of £205,999.[41] When Norman Macleod of Macleod finally became insolvent in 1849 his assets totalled £100, 027 and his debts £106,851.[42]

There is no denying the fact that examples of reckless overspending do exist in the historical record. In such cases a family's fortune and position in society could be irreparably damaged by the behaviour of irresponsible individuals. Two classic instances of this type were Charles Maclean of Drimnin in Morvern, 'a careless, imprudent and extravagant man', who sold the family property in bankruptcy in 1797-8 and the sixth Duke of Argyll, 'a notorious rake and outrageous spendthrift', who managed single-handedly to reduce the family fortune by £2 million.[43] But one must avoid the conclusion that these individuals were necessarily typical of the Highland landed class as a whole and, more importantly, that it was the inadequacy of certain landlords and the debts they accumulated which are the fundamental factors explaining the large number of forced sales which occurred in the western Highlands in this period. There are a number of problems with such an interpretation. First, financial failure and distress were common among most landed families in the region. This suggests that they faced common problems and difficulties in the economic and social environment rather than that their position was weakened by the behaviour of aberrant individuals. It is possible that some families may have found themselves under the authority and control of inadequate life-tenants in these years; it is much less likely, however, that the vast majority of the landed class suddenly found themselves in a similarly unfortunate position. Second, large debts in themselves were not new. Dr. Shaw's work on the seventeenth-century Highlands shows that indebtedness was very common among most west Highland proprietors at that time.[44] It was debt, for example, which led to the downfall of the Macleans of Duart in 1674 and the transfer of their lands to the Campbell Earls of Argyll. Nor were the sums owed negligible. To cite but one example, an account of Clanranald's debts to Macdonald of Sleat in 1700 indicates that they stood at £64,000.[45] Such amounts were by no means exceptional. What requires explanation in the nineteenth century, therefore, is not so much the extent of debt in itself but why (unlike the pattern in previous periods) it apparently precipitated such a massive increase in sales of land.

Third, it cannot be assumed that the incidence of debt in itself necessarily implied overspending or financial weakness. As F.M.L. Thompson has put it, 'Debts require careful handling as evidence: they may as easily indicate increasing prosperity as increasing adversity, intelligent use of available resources as wayward appropriation'.[46] A survey of the estate papers of Lord Macdonald, Macleod of Macleod and Sir James Riddell reveals that some debt was incurred for reasons of conspicuous consumption, such as the improvement of estate mansions, the building of town houses and the purchasing of fine furniture. But it is equally clear that much also derived from unsuccessful investments in the infrastructure of the estate and in the provision of relief for destitute tenants during bad seasons.[47] The Riddell family, for instance, sunk more than £52,000 in their Ardnamurchan and Sunart estates in 'buildings, roads, enclosure, drainage' between 1818 and 1848 which then failed to bring the expected returns.[48]

Fourth, it is unhistorical to separate the Highland elite from the British landed class as a whole and then evaluate their social behaviour and spending patterns on the implicit or explicit assumption that they were a different breed, inhabiting a different social world, with different responsibilities and expectations. This is too common an error in Scottish historical studies. From at least as early as the seventeenth century, the Highland landed class had been accustomed to moving in two cultural universes, the tribal world of the north and the polite society of the south. By the end of the eighteenth century, their values, intellectual assumptions and material tastes were little different from those of their peers in central and southern Scotland and the rest of Britain. They were unlikely to be able to escape the powerful and irresistible social pressures which permeated British landed society in the age of the Revolution of Manners. This was the era of competitive emulation when position in elite society was judged not by the size of a traditional following or by inherited family prestige but by the material symbols of status and authority such as housing, dress and style of life.[49] It would have been impossible for Highland landowners to insulate themselves from these changes in fashion and spending. To have done so would have meant the surrender of their place in society and the abrogation of their very membership of the British social elite. In the Regency age increased conspicuous consumption was synonymous with the very status of a great landowner.[50] Highland proprietors, like all others, were therefore encouraged to raise income from their estates to accommodate the material standards of the new era.

This last point brings the argument to the very core of the problem. The key factor in the survival of financially embarrassed families was not so much the level of debt alone but the balance between debt and income. Disaster loomed only when the cost of servicing annual interest charges became equal to or even greater than annual income.[51] It was here that west Highland landowners were most at risk. Historians of the British landed classes argue that it was exceedingly difficult for land-owners to reduce absolute debt levels even through the imposition of strict measures of economy.[52] This was because much debt was inher-ited and a considerable amount of income was tied up in servicing the interest charges associated with earlier loans and mortgages. Further-more, each estate was burdened with an array of annuities, life-rents, jointures and portions for different members of the landed family other than the life-tenant. The convention of primogeniture meant that it became customary to make allowances to younger sons and daughters which became fixed and unavoidable charges on estate income. The composition of Lord Macdonald's debt of over £140,000 in 1846 was entirely typical of those other Highland proprietors. £84,489, or 60 per cent of the total sum, was inherited from his father and grandfather and £56,187 was incurred during his lifetime. He had a gross annual income of £11,269 but only £3298 of this was 'free', the rest being absorbed in interest payments and other charges.[53] Similarly, in 1826, 83 per cent of the Earl of Seaforth's annual rental of £7087 from his Lewis estate was absorbed in the payment of interest.[54] It followed, therefore, that without spectacular increases in revenue from land sales or significant increases in estate income it was difficult, if not impossible, to substantially reduce levels of inherited debt. There were several instances of land being sold to increase revenue and, in some cases, these actions did stabilise the situation.[55] But the pressures were so inexorable and insidious that the respite, especially for smaller landowners, was often only temporary. Thus Macleod of Macleod cleared off all his father's debts and also obtained a 'reversion' of about £30,000 after selling off Glenelg in 1810 for £100,000. By 1820 he had 'a clear, unencumbered estate' which yielded £9,000 a year.[56] Less than three decades later, however, the family's properties were being run by trustees for the family's creditors. Only a combination of stable or increasing levels of income, lower annual costs and sound estate management could have saved the Highland landed class. In the event, however, the first two of these factors were missing, and some would argue that even the third was also absent. The hereditary elite of the society was therefore doomed.

The economic cycle which precipitated bankruptcies and land sales in the aftermath of the Napoleonic Wars has been well documented.[57] In the period 1790 to 1812 money flooded into the Highlands as a result of the spectacular increases in cattle prices, the windfall gains from kelping, and additional income from sheep-farming, fishing and illicit distillation. Rent rolls on all west Highland estates swelled as proprietors creamed off the increasing returns from these varied economic activities. Then, just as dramatically, prosperity ebbed away in the 1820s with the collapse of kelp manufacture, the slump in cattle prices and the malaise in the fisheries. The great land sales of this period were one result of this economic crisis as deflationary pressures forced those with high fixed charges based on wartime levels of income to unload their properties on to the market. The story is a familiar one but it does not in itself entirely explain the unique and unprecedented scale of land trans-

fers in the western Highlands or why debt should have had a more devastating effect in the region in this period than in previous centuries.

The majority of British landowners had to contend with a more difficult economic environment by the 1820s but the position of west Highland proprietors was probably more critical and insecure than most.
For one thing, even in the years of high prosperity, many estates
remained so debt-encumbered that ' . . . the first breath of falling rents
was sufficient to sweep them on to the market'.[58] Increased income,
ephemeral though it was, was not sufficient to overcome the central
problem of the old west Highland elite: the difficulty, or perhaps even
the impossibility, of maintaining the material standards now necessary
to ensure full participation in the life of the British landed class on the
relatively paltry returns from a poor land, an insecure economy and an
impoverished peasantry. Highland proprietors socialised with southern landlords, many of whom increasingly depended on the fruits of
urban expansion and mineral royalties to sustain a higher standard of
living. These were not available to most Highland landowners. They
could not compete. But in trying to do so they probably left themselves
more vulnerable to the postwar recession than their counterparts in
other regions of Britain.

But that recession in the western Highlands was also more
devastating in its effects than the contemporaneous fall in agricultural
prices which occurred in lowland Scotland. There the depression
caused difficulty and lowered income as rents fell and abatements were
awarded to hard-pressed tenant farmers.[59] But it did not produce a
crisis. Mixed farming in the Lowlands allowed for adjustment to a
different market structure; the price of oats and barley, staples in the
Scottish countryside, fell only moderately compared to wheat, which
was cultivated widely only in some parts, and continued industrial and
urban expansion allowed many proprietors to tap non-agricultural
sources of income.[60] It was a quite different story in the western
Highlands. As prices fell, marginal economic areas invariably suffered
most. The vital point is that *all* sectors of this regional economy were in
difficulty. Hence, there was little opportunity for manoeuvre or for the
implementation of policies which might temper the worst effects of the
recession. Each one of the wartime supports of the economy crumbled
in the years after Waterloo. Cattle prices halved between 1810 and 1830;
the halcyon days of the herring fishery on the north-west coast came
abruptly to an end and success returned only intermittently from the
1820s. Even sheep prices declined on trend. Blackface wethers were selling at an average of 19.0s between 1818 and 1822. By 1828-32, the price
had fallen to 15.2s. Laid Cheviot wool sold at 11.6 pence per lb. from 1818

E

to 1822. From 1828 to 1832, prices slumped to 6.3 pence per lb.[61] But the most serious crisis came from the collapse of kelping. It sank to unprofitable levels in most areas by the later 1820s. It was, therefore, no coincidence that it was the two greatest kelp landlords, Macdonald of Clanranald and Mackenzie of Seaforth, who were among the first to lose their lands in the postwar era. The manufacture of kelp had come to dominate the economy of their estates and they inevitably suffered the consequences of such risky over-specialisation when the bottom fell out of the market in the 1820s. As late as 1826, for example, by which time the proceeds of kelp had already declined considerably, they still made up 53 per cent of the total Seaforth rental on Lewis of £7953.[62]

The immediate consequence of the price collapse was a dramatic surge in rent arrears and hence a sharp fall in the disposable income required to service debt charges.[63] Because rentals had been raised to cream off most of the peasant income in return for the possession of land, arrears inevitably began to accumulate as soon as prices faltered. The proprietor had often to bear the full brunt of the contraction because in the kelping estates the population 'paid' rent in the form of labouring in the industry while the 'wage' consisted of meal supplies and land provided by the landowner. Yet, while income from kelp shrank, several proprietors had still to maintain the traditional obligation to supply meal which became even more pressing in such years of harvest failure as 1816-17, 1821-2, 1825, 1836-7 and, above all, during the great potato famine of 1846 to 1856.[64] At these times, in particular, arrears spiralled as relief costs rose. Several proprietors were therefore caught in a seemingly inescapable vice between contraction in income and stubbornly high, or even on occasion, rising costs.[65] Evidence from estate papers demonstrates both the pain inflicted by this crisis and the desperate measures which were taken to try and retrieve the situation. Land sales, financial retrenchment, negotiations of fresh loans, changes in land use (particularly conversion of croft lands to sheep farming), were all attempted. In many cases, however, they merely postponed the inevitable.

One reason why they were generally ineffective was that the financial and market environment in which nineteenth-century Highland landowners had to live was radically different from that of their predecessors of the seventeenth century. Then, too, as has been seen, indebtedness was common. But despite the heavy debts of many of the landowners in the Western Isles, very few estates changed hands or were broken up before 1700.[66] Two factors possibly help to explain the different consequences of indebtedness in the two periods. The first of these was the changing sources of credit. In the seventeenth century, the overwhelming majority of loans were obtained from kinsmen, vassals or close associates usually in the form of a wadset, a pledge of lands in security for a debt. It would appear that such arrangements rarely resulted in forfeiture or annexation of lands from the debtor even when he was in dire financial straits. This has been explained in terms of the strong sense of kin-loyalty which existed between debtor and creditor, a relationship cemented by hereditary attachment to the family lands and the influence of the ancient Celtic kin-based social structure which ensured that the loyalty of the kindred group focused on its ruling family.[67]

However, the social and economic context of borrowing and lending had fundamentally altered by the early nineteenth century. The expansion of landed debt which occurred in the later eighteenth-century Highlands was simply a regional variant of a British phenomenon. It now became much easier to borrow as a result of the growth of the banking system, the advent of the insurance companies, secular decline in the rate of interest and legal changes which rendered it easier for landowners to obtain credit.[68] From the 1770s, for instance, landed estates became acceptable security for bankers' advances in Scotland. The wartime prosperity of agriculture boosted the attraction of providing mortgages on landed property while the postwar slump in the yield of Consols stimulated insurance companies in particular to lend vast sums on the security of land. One could even speculate, although confirmation from original evidence is hard to obtain, that the debts of Highland proprietors may be due as much to the ease with which money could now be borrowed from a wide range of sources as to their own individual patterns of consumption and expenditure.

An analysis of the long-term loans owed by Lord Macdonald in 1846 illustrates the changes which had occurred since the seventeenth century.[69] Only £19,542, or about 14 per cent of the sums owed, were due to creditors with Highland surnames. Only 2 per cent were owed to individuals with the surname Macdonald. Lord Macdonald's grandfather had owed 15 per cent of his debt to creditors of that name. On the other hand, of the total debt in 1846 of £140,676, over £37,600 were owed to trust funds and a further £20,637 to banks and insurance companies. In the short term, this flow of credit from the savings of the Lowland upper and middle classes and institutions helped to raise the standard of living of Highland proprietors and was an important (if unacknowledged) source of subsidy to the west Highland economy as a whole.[70] But in the long term, its results were more ambiguous because southern lawyers and bankers were likely to be less sympathetic to the plight of embarrassed debtors than the kinsman creditors of earlier times. This formalised and impersonal credit structure made it more probable that default on annual interest payments would not easily be permitted. Creditors were likely to appoint trustees to supervise the administration of properties in difficulty and, when deemed necessary, sell off lands to protect the value of their securities.[71]

The second factor facilitating land sales in this period was the changing nature of the market for Highland property. In the seventeenth century, the purchase of west Highland land by outsiders was rare in the extreme. The absence of demand therefore doubtless also helps to explain the slow turnover of estates in that period. Creditors were perhaps less inclined to foreclose when the 'market' value of the asset against which their loan was secured was in doubt. By the middle decades of the nineteenth century, however, this artificial insulation of debtors from the rigours of the market had come to an end. Highland estates were in great demand from social groups outside the Highlands who often had the resources to pay considerably more for them than the asking price. Creditors were now likely to be much keener to force sales. The great transfers of Highland property which occurred in this period were, therefore, not simply due to an increase in the supply of estates to the market but of augmented demand which itself accelerated the release of much territory for sale.

3

The new interest which developed in the acquisition of Highland property from the 1820s is in one sense paradoxical and ironic. Despite the economic and social crisis which became acute at this time, land prices rose as never before and the west Highland region began to attract very wealthy purchasers, not only from the Scottish Lowlands but from further afield. As one commentator observed in 1848: 'Look at the whole stretch of country from Fort Augustus to Fort William and Arisaig in the possession of rich English capitalists . . .'.[72] There can be little doubt of the new market potential of Highland estates. When property was put up for sale, the final price was frequently significantly higher than the original upset price. Glentronie in Badenoch was sold in 1835 to Henry Baillie, a wealthy Bristol West India merchant, for £7350, over £2000 above the upset price.[73] The Cromartie lands of Fannich and Lochbroom in Ross-shire were advertised at £13,150 in 1835, but fetched £17,700.[74] Barra was 'exposed to sale' for £36,000 in 1839 but was eventually purchased by James Menzies for over £42,000.[75] Several other examples exist of this pattern. They all confirm the buoyancy of demand for Highland property.[76] When an estate was put on the market, considerable competition from prospective purchasers could be anticipated. Glengarry, for example, attracted 'many offers'and the sale price rose as a result from £88,000 until the property was finally acquired in 1840 for £91,000 by Lord Ward.[77]

Even in periods of acute crisis in the western Highlands, there was little indication that the land market was adversely affected. A clutch of estates was released for sale in 1838-9 in the aftermath of the serious harvest failures of 1836-7 but they all quickly obtained ready purchasers.[78] During the great potato famine of 1846 to 1856, when the population of entire districts was plunged into destitution, it still proved possible to successfully market property in the stricken region. The estate of Lynedale in Skye, in the very heart of the famine zone, was acquired for £9000 by Alexander Macdonald of Thornbank near Falkirk in the summer of 1849 at an advance of 10 per cent higher than the price it fetched when sold in 1838.[79] Larger properties did prove more difficult to sell but even they eventually found purchasers. The Islay estate was advertised in 1848 for £540,000 but had to be lowered to £451,000 before it was bought four years later by James Morrison of Basildon Park. But the trustees did not have to split up the estate into separate lots to facilitate a sale and, in the event, Morrison only acquired Islay after the intervention of James Baird (of the great Scottish coal and iron manufacturing dynasty) which pushed up the sale price from £440,000 to £451,000.[80] Indeed, what is especially interesting about this pattern of demand for Highland property is that it did not apparently fluctuate in accordance either with trends in the national land market or with the vicissitudes of the national economy. The exchange of Highland estates increased between c.1820 and c.1860 and did not suffer the temporary recession in the 1830s and 1840s which seems to have occurred elsewhere.[81] This suggests that there were particular factors influencing demand and supply of Highland land which did not operate to the same extent in other parts of the country.

In the very broadest sense, the development can be seen as one important manifestation of the evolution of pronounced regional specialisation within the British economy in the nineteenth century. The economic plight of the Highlands in the generation or two after Waterloo derived to a large extent from the adverse impact of competition and demand from the dynamic industrial economy of the rest of Britain. It was the advanced manufacturing centres and improved agricultural regions to the south and east which undercut the marginal producers of the western Highlands and islands, destroyed the infant industrial growth points of the wartime era and converted the region into a source of wool, mutton and cheap labour for the rest of the Scottish economy. The process of economic growth itself, therefore, created a chronic regional imbalance which in simple terms can be viewed as the development of an impoverished north and west and a relatively prosperous Lowland economy. In the latter zone, enormous surpluses emerged, concentrated in the possession of the wealthy entrepreneurial and rentier classes, which were then redeployed in the purchase of land now more available in the north because of the economic disasters which had overwhelmed the Highland region. In this interpretation, therefore, the emergence of a new elite was simply one inevitable consequence of the dependent and weakened position of Highland society. It was a confirmation of its satellite status. Highland estates served the needs of the affluent of the south in the same way that the region's pastoral farms and teeming populations served the economic requirements of southern cities and industries. The result was ' . . . a remarkable juxtaposition of some of the most successful entrepreneurs of the Victorian age with the least modernised agrarian margin'.[82]

There is much force in this argument and it forms the essential economic background for an understanding of the broad forces which were at work. But it alone does not adequately explain the extraordinary surge in demand for Highland property which persisted even when the general economic context was far from propitious. It is interesting to note, for example, that while Walter Campbell's trustees managed to sell Islay in 1852, they were still attempting to get rid of Woodhall, his other estate in Lanarkshire, as late as 1854 and this despite the fact that the property, 'the great proportion of the value of which consists of minerals', lay in the very centre of the booming industrial area of west-central Scotland.[83] It was apparently the Highland estate, with its famine-stricken population and low rental, which proved more attractive to purchasers than the lands in Lanarkshire which were richly endowed with coal and iron-ore measures and situated close to manufacturing industry. This example clearly indicates the peculiar attraction which the acquisition of Highland property now had for many of the affluent classes in Victorian Britain.

The purchase of landed estates in general, and perhaps in particular land in the Highlands in the nineteenth century, hardly seems to reflect rational economic self-interest. Agricultural land, even in rich farming counties, yielded little more than an annual return of 2.5 to 3.5 per cent, which was substantially less than the dividends which could be earned in other forms of investment.[84] The great value of landed property was not therefore in its profitability but rather in its permanence. It was not only a secure investment but also provided a passive source of rentier income. Philip Gaskell has shown that in Morvern in Argyllshire several small estates were acquired in the nineteenth century by owners who rarely if ever visited them and simply extracted rental as a secure and dependable income.[85] The value of Highland property for these purposes had increased with the clearance of small tenants, the massive growth in sheep farming and the expansion of deer forests. In Inverness-shire, the total number of sheep rose from 154,000 in 1811 to 542,000 in 1854; in Ross-shire from 50,946 to 251,619 and in Sutherland from 37,130 to 162,103.[86] Sheep farms not only yielded regular rentals but they were also more easily collected by local factors for the owner and these increased on trend as prices for wool and mutton rose from the later 1840s to the early 1870s. Many small properties in Mull and Morvern in particular, where estates were considerably divided, also attracted owners who were not much interested in experiencing the life and status of a landed gentleman but rather in establishing a secure source of investment.[87]

Others saw land purchase in the Highlands as a means of making capital gains. As demand for estates developed, speculators exploited the opportunity of buying land in a rising market and selling later at a handsome profit. The island of Harris was sold for £60,000 in 1831; half of it was converted to deer and in 1871 fetched £155,000. Lord Hill bought part of Applecross in 1860 for £76,000. After spending £14,000 on it he was able to resell it for £191,000.[88] The crucial economic background to these speculative gains was the boom in sheep prices in the 1850s and 1860s and the inflation in sporting rents which began in the same period. In a more risky position were those who bought for 'economic' reasons in earlier decades when sheep prices were relatively stagnant and the sporting economy was in its infancy. Even in the 1830s and 1840s, however, there were those who imagined that they could achieve considerable returns by purchasing encumbered Highland estates and transforming them into highly profitable assets by investing in them and assiduously applying the techniques of Lowland 'improvement' to their administration. This was a basic reason why the acquisition of some Highland estates by outsiders was sometimes followed very quickly by the clearance and forced emigration of the small tenantry who were viewed as one of the major economic obstacles to profitability. This was the predictable outcome when the Stirling lawyer, Francis Clark, bought Ulva; after the purchase of Raasay by George Rainy; when several estates in Mull and Morvern were acquired by new owners; and above all, when John Gordon of Cluny bought Barra, South Uist and Benbecula.[89]

The very cheapness of Highland land, relative to other areas of Scotland and England, posed both a challenge and an opportunity to these men. They bought partly *because* rentals were low and the land was poor in the hope of transforming its prospects and so making huge gains in the long term. Gordon of Cluny is a classic case.[90] He died possessed of property worth £2 to £3 millions, 'without doubt the richest commoner in Scotland'. In his obituary his interest in land purchase was explained by the fact that he was ' . . .dissatisfied . . . at the returns obtained in the way of interest and dividends'. Gordon was an extremely hard-headed businessman who undertook very careful supervision of his properties, ' . . .nearly every receipt of rent . . . being signed by his own hand'. He was far from being a naive visionary who rashly hoped to transform barren acres into fertile soil. His acquisition of the Uists was part of a much wider programme of estate purchase and improvement which ended when he became the owner of vast properties in Aberdeenshire, Banff, Nairn and Midlothian as well as in the Hebrides. However, speculation in the Uists was spectacularly unsuccessful. By 1848, he had obtained less then ⅔ per cent return on his capital and had had to lay out nearly £8000 on famine relief for the people of his estates. In 1847 arrears stood at £14,500 and the annual rental of £8223 at the time of purchase had to be reduced to £4894. However, the intervention of Gordon, and others like him who bought on a more modest scale, is a reminder that there were 'rational' economic reasons for Highland land purchase at this time even if the optimistic assumptions on which they were based sometimes proved to be false.

It would be quite wrong, on the other hand, to give the impression that the majority of new estate owners acquired Highland property to maximise economic returns or to obtain secure and permanent assets. These elements were relevant in several cases but they were not generally decisive nor do they adequately explain why Highland land became so much more marketable in the nineteenth century than it had ever been in the past. To deal effectively with this question it is necessary to take a wider view. In essence, it seems to have been a direct consequence of a revolutionary change in the perception of the western Highlands and islands on the part of the affluent and leisured classes of British society in Victorian times. Before the middle of the eighteenth century, the region was viewed by external observers as a barren and sterile wilderness, inhabited by a barbarous population, many of whom were disaffected to the British crown. By the early decades of the century, a transformation had taken place.[91] The revolution in taste associated with the Romantic Movement, the new interest in Nature, and the rise of the ideas of the sublime and the picturesque, all served to create a wholly new response to the physical features of the Highlands.

Truly 'modern' attitudes to scenic beauty were born; the wilderness became invested with qualities of romance and imbued with historical, legendary and traditional associations. The western Highlands became an area (like the Lake District) where it was now possible to commune with nature and achieve spiritual renewal and restful solitude in an atmosphere of other-worldly isolation. The former disadvantages of the region, its relative inaccessibility and wild character, became points of positive attraction rather than features which repelled and disgusted.

It is difficult to wholly appreciate the enormous appeal which the 'romantic' Highlands had for the British upper and middle classes by the 1840s. In 1853, for instance, the *Illustrated London News* described how 'The desolate grandeur of the scenery of Skye annually attracts to it crowds of tourists. Every phase of our society is duly represented in the course of each season, at the Stor, Quirang, Coruisk, and the Cuchuillin or Coollen Hills. They returned delighted as well they may, with the wildest and most impressive scenery in the kingdom'.[92] Another observer around the same time pointed to the irresistible attraction of the Highlands for the rich and famous:

> Within the last forty years scarcely one of any note in the world of letters that has not left footprints on Benledie, Benlomand, Benevis, and Cairn Gorum, and wandered by the lakes and scenes rendered dear to heart and eye by the songs and stories of Ossian and Scott; while the most celebrated of these classic scenes have been transferred to canvas by the pencils of Williams, Landseer, MacCulloch and others the first artists of the age.

> Instead of wandering on the banks of the Rhine, the Med., the Missilonghi, the Tiber, the Po and the Seine, which formerly formed the grand tour . . . a visit of some weeks' duration to the mountains and rivers of the Tay, the Dee, the Avon, the Spey, the Caledonian Canal and the Western Islands now constitutes the grand tour of fashionable life.[93]

It was in this period, too, that the region developed as a major centre for the physical sports of hunting, shooting and fishing. The *Inverness Courier* concluded as early as 1835 that 'Even unconquerable barrenness is now turned to good account. At the present moment, we believe, many Highland proprietors derive a greater revenue from their moors alone, for grouse shooting, than their whole rental amounted to sixty years since'.[94] 28 deer forests were formed before 1839; a further 16 were established in the 1840s, 10 in the early 1850s and a further 18 between 1855 and 1860.[95] The greatest expansion only came after 1880 but already by the middle decades of the nineteenth century there had been substantial development. The comment made in 1892 that ' . . . as soon as a man has amassed a fortune in any way his first desire seems to be to buy or hire a deer forest in Scotland and there to gather his friends to enjoy his hospitality and sport' also has much relevance for earlier decades.[96]

The precondition both for the vast expansion in Highland tourism and the rise of the sporting economy was the revolution in communications. The western Highlands throughout this period possessed the unique qualities of 'remoteness' and isolation which were an integral part of its magical appeal for Victorians. But the region was no longer inaccessible. New transport facilities guaranteed reasonably quick and comfortable connections from the great urban centres in the south. The pathbreaking development was the invention of the ocean-going paddle steamer which for the first time brought a reliable and regular transport system to the Western Isles and the lochs of the western mainland.[97] By the 1840s 'a bridge of boats' securely linked the Clyde to the Hebrides.[98] Equally significant in other areas was the revolution in road transport. Coach services radically improved. In 1836 it was said, with some astonishment, that 'a person might now dine in Edinburgh one day, and breakfast in Inverness the next'. Twenty years before the journey had taken four days.[99] In the later 1830s the Caledonian coach left Edinburgh three times a week, ' . . . crowded with tourists, and their baggage, a motley catalogue of guns, fishing rods, pointers, creels and baskets'.[100]

The transport revolution was both cause and effect of the new importance assumed by the western Highlands in the recreational pursuits of the Victorian middle and upper classes. The *Inverness Courier* reported that 'The passion entertained by English gentlemen for field sports has been fostered by increased means of communication northward and up and down the country, from the highest hill to the deepest and most distant glen. The sportsman throws himself into a steamer at London and in 48 hours or less he is in Edinburgh or Aberdeen. Another day and he is in the heart of moor and mountain, where he may shoot, saunter or angle to his heart's content'.[101] But the appeal of the region was not simply confined to those who sought to kill for pleasure. All the leisure interests of the affluent classes were catered for. The new tourists not only consisted of 'sportsmen with dogs and guns' but also 'the geologist with his bag and hammer, the botanist with his book of specimens, the scene hunter with his pencil and numerous groups intent only on picnicking among wild hills, streams or waterfalls'.[102]

Only a handful of those who swarmed into the Highlands, carried by the steamships and faster coaches in the middle decades of the nineteenth century, could hope to aspire to estate ownership. But the attractions which now enticed the many into the region were also those which stimulated the few to purchase land. It was the 'glamour' of the western Highlands which encouraged Octavius Smith, the wealthy London distiller, to buy the estate which was eventually named Ardtornish in Morvern and to erect an elaborate mansion on it as a 'holiday home'.[103] In 1845, the Marquis of Salisbury purchased the island of Rhum for £24,000 to develop it as a deer forest.[104] Sir Dudley Marjoribanks, later Lord Tweedsmouth, acquired Guisachan in Strathglass in 1854 for £52,000 for the same reason.[105] Duncan Darroch's purchase of Torridon in 1872 was stimulated by his desire to 'enjoy the sport I love so well, the noblest sport of all, deer stalking'.[106]

But the exceptional availability of Highland estates also helped to satisfy other more powerful psychological drives and needs among the wealthy. Recent research has demonstrated how it was difficult even for the most affluent members of the new merchant and industrialist classes to buy a great deal of land in Victorian times.[107] This was not necessarily because of their lack of desire to do so but rather because few large estates ever came to market and such land as was available for sale was usually extremely expensive.[108] In the western Highlands, however, extensive areas of land were not only available for purchase from the 1820s but, in relative terms at least, they were cheap. In the 1870s, the owners of the Arisaig estate also possessed territory in Cheshire. The Arisaig lands had a gross annual value of only £0.07 per acre whereas the Cheshire property was valued at £3.7 per acre. The Marquis of Northampton's Mull estate was reckoned to be worth £0.15 per acre while his estates in Warwick were valued at £1 per acre.[109] It was possible, therefore, for successful businessmen to buy up many thousands of acres in the north-west for an outlay which would have afforded them only a small country estate in most other regions of Britain. It mattered not that much of the land was useless because its main function may have been simply to satisfy the urge for territorial possession. It became a form of conspicuous consumption, a means by which material success could be demonstrated, status and place in society assured and a family line established. In this sense, buying a Highland estate and 'improving' it gratified the same passion for possession as the collection of fine art or the acquisition of expensive and elaborate furniture.

Those men who obtained Highland land in such great quantities could afford to indulge themselves because they were among the very wealthiest in Britain. James Morrison, who acquired Islay, for example, has been described as 'possibly the richest British commoner in the nineteenth century'.[110] But perhaps the most extraordinary examples of extravagance in territorial acquisition came from the activities of Alexander (later Sir Alexander) Matheson and his kinsman, Sir James Matheson.[111] Both had amassed huge fortunes in the lucrative China trade and returned to Britain in their middle years to establish landed families. Each was drawn to the country of his ancestors. James was the son of an officer in the Earl of Sutherland's fencible regiments. Alexander's family were from Lochalsh. His father had owned the estate of Attadale but had had to sell it because of insolvency in 1825. On his return from the East, James Matheson purchased two small estates in his native Sutherland in 1840 and then obtained the island of Lewis in 1844 from the bankrupt Earls of Seaforth. Over the following two decades he spent substantially more than a quarter of a million pounds on a wide range of land improvements, additions to the island's infrastructure and support for the fisheries. Alexander indulged in an even more spectacular spending spree. With his 'magnificent fortune', he acquired six separate estates in Lochalsh and Kintail, including the former lands of his family, at a total cost of £238,020. A further outlay of over £185,000 was used to purchase property in Easter Ross. By 1870, he owned territory of more than 220,000 acres in extent, an area which yielded only just over £23,000 in annual rent but made him a greater Highland landowner in terms of territory possessed than such grandees as the Duke of Atholl or the Duke of Argyll. During his lifetime, £400,000 was spent, in addition to the purchase price of his estates, on improvement to his properties and on the building and furnishing of mansion houses.

Matheson was the apotheosis of one type of new landowner in the Highlands, an individual of colossal wealth who lavished expenditure on his estates and in the process helped to subsidise the local economy from the profits of trade earned in distant and exotic parts of the world. The activities of men like him ensured that the drain of rental income from the Highlands, which had occurred when the old elite expended much of the surplus of their estates in the fashionable capitals of the south, was now reversed. Instead, the new landed class spent much of the profit derived from their commercial and professional success outside the Highlands in the north and west. This must have made a significant contribution in some localities to the economic recovery which took place in the crofting region in the aftermath of the potato famine of the middle decades of the nineteenth century.

NOTES

This essay is partly based on research derived from a wider project on the nineteenth-century Highlands funded by the Economic and Social Research Council (Grant No. B00232099) and the University of Strathclyde Research and Development Fund in 1985 and 1986. I am most grateful to the Council and the University for their generous support and to my research assistant, Mr. W. Orr, for his help in the collection of data. Acknowledgement is made to the following for permission to consult and cite original material: the Keeper of the Records of Scotland; the Keeper and Trustees of the National Library of Scotland; the Duke of Argyll; Donald Cameron of Lochiel; John Macleod of Macleod; John Mackenzie of Gairloch.

1. See, *inter alia*, James Hunter, *The Making of the Crofting Community* (Edinburgh, 1976); J.M. Bumstead, *The People's Clearance: Highland Emigration to British North America 1770-1815* (Edinburgh, 1982); Eric Richards, *A History of the Highland Clearances*, Volumes 1 and 2 (London, 1982, 1985); T.M. Devine, *The Great Highland Famine: Hunger, Emigration and the Scottish Highlands in the Nineteenth Century* (Edinburgh, 1988); A.J. Youngson, *After the Forty Five* (Edinburgh, 1973).

2. But see Philip Gaskell, *Morvern Transformed* (Cambridge, 1968); E.R. Cregeen, 'The Changing Role of the House of Argyll in the Scottish Highlands', in N.T. Phillipson and Rosalind Mitchison, eds., *Scotland in the Age of Improvement* (Edinburgh, 1970); Eric Richards, *The Leviathan of Wealth* (London, 1973); R.J. Adam, ed., *Papers on Sutherland Estate Management*, 2 volumes (Edinburgh, 1972).

3. The most penetrating studies have been undertaken of the two ducal families of Argyll and Sutherland but apart from Philip Gaskell's survey of landlords in the Argyllshire parish of Morvern little has been published on the mass of middling and smaller proprietors.

4. J. Mitchell, *Reminiscences of my Life in the Highlands* (London, 1883-4), II, p.114.

5. Unless otherwise indicated, all generalisations rely on information contained in the Appendix.

6. Scottish Record Office (SRO), Campbell of Jura Papers, GD64/1/347, Report to the Creditors of the late Walter F. Campbell.

7. W.C. Mackenzie, *History of the Outer Hebrides* (Paisley, 1903), pp.493-6.

8. J. Barron, *The Northern Highlands in the Nineteenth Century* (Inverness, 1907), II, pp.329-330.

9. Dunvegan Castle, Macleod of Macleod Muniments, 3/838, N. Macleod to General Kyd, 6 February, 1820; National Library of Scotland (NLS), Sutherland Estate Papers, Dep. 313/1174, James Loch to Duke of Sutherland, 8 March, 1847; *Scotsman*, 15 September, 1847; 3 July, 1850; SRO, Lord Macdonald Papers, GD221/43, Report by Mr. Balingall for Mr. Brown, 1851. Macleod offered for sale in 1847 Grishernish (5000 acres) at £13,000 and Glendale (14,231 acres) at £35,000.

10. Barron, *Northern Highlands*, II, pp.329-330; *Parliamentary Papers*, (*PP*), *Report to the Board of Supervision by Sir John McNeill*, XXVI (1851), p.XV.

11. Gaskell, *Morvern Transformed*, pp.23-24.

12. John Bateman, *The Great Landowners of Great Britain and Ireland* (London, 1882).

13. The generalisations which follow are based on Frances J. Shaw, *The Northern and Western Islands of Scotland: Their Economy and Society in the Seventeenth Century* (Edinburgh, 1980), pp.16-30. L. Timperley, 'The Pattern of Landholding in Eighteenth Century Scotland', in M.L. Parry and T.R. Slater, eds., *The Making of the Scottish Countryside* (London, 1980), pp.137-154; L. Timperley, 'Landownership

in Scotland in the Eighteenth Century', unpublished Ph.D. thesis, University of Edinburgh, 1977.

14. J. Smith, *General View of the Agriculture of the County of Argyll* (London, 1805), p.14.

15. Margaret D. Storrie, *Islay: Biography of an Island* (Port Ellen, 1981), pp.58-9. Even the Campbells could not strictly be described as 'non-Highland'. Daniel Campbell made his fortune in transatlantic trade, but he was the second son of Walter Campbell, Captain of Skipness in Argyll, and his mother had Islay connections.

16. *PP, McNeill Report* (1851), p.XV.

17. Inevitably some of these distinctions are rather arbitrary. Some 'landowners' had either business interests or had bought into land with the profits of trade. 'Merchants' had industrial interests and 'manufacturers' had commercial connections.

18. Entries in *Inverness Courier*, 1813-38.

19. A. Fullarton and C.R. Baird, *Remarks on the Evils at Present affecting the Highlands and Islands of Scotland* (Glasgow, 1838), pp.45-6; *Scotsman*, 23 August, 1837; *New Statistical Account of Scotland* (Edinburgh, 1835-45) (N.S.A.), XIV, p.195.

20. Storrie, *Islay*, pp.141-160.

21. Shaw, *Northern and Western Islands*, p.19: *PP, McNeill Report* (1851), p.XV.

22. Bateman, *Great Landowners, passim*.

23. For the British land market, see F.M.L. Thompson, 'The Land Market in the Nineteenth Century', *Oxford Economic Papers*, 2nd ser., 9 (1957), pp.268-308.

24. *Ibid.*, p.293.

25. Lawrence Stone and Jeanne C. Fautier Stone, *An Open Elite? England 1540-1880* (Oxford, 1984), esp. Chs. vi-viii; W.D. Rubinstein, *Men of Property* (London, 1981) and 'New Men of Wealth and the Purchase of Land in Nineteenth Century England', *Past and Present*, 92 (1981), pp.127-140. There was a similar pattern in parts of Lowland Scotland. Of the 106 owners with lands valued at £1,500 per annum and more in Aberdeenshire in 1872, only 12 had acquired their estates in the previous fifty years. See R.F. Callander, *A Pattern of Landownership in Scotland* (Finzean, 1987), pp.70-1.

26. Rubinstein, 'New Men of Wealth', p.131.

27. F.M.L. Thompson, *English Landed Society in the Nineteenth Century* (London, 1963), Ch. 12; David Cannadine, 'Aristocratic Indebtedness in the Nineteenth Century: the Case Re-Opened', *Economic History Review*, 2nd ser., XXX (November, 1977), pp.645-649.

28. David Spring, 'The English Landed Estate in the Age of Coal and Iron: 1830-80', *Journal of Economic History*, XI (1951), p.16.

29. SRO, Loch Muniments, GD268/224, Lady Stafford to James Loch, 1 December 1832.

30. SRO, Campbell of Jura Papers, GD64/1/347, Report to the Creditors of the late Walter F. Campbell of Islay.

31. SRO, Clanranald Papers, GD201/5/1223, Macdonald of Clanranald to John Gordon, 2 December 1839; Richards, *Highland Clearances*, II, p.462.

32. See Appendix.

33. Dunvegan Castle, Macleod of Macleod Muniments, Section 3/838; N. Macleod (?) to General Kyd, 6 February 1820; SRO, Lord Macdonald Papers, GD221/1856/3, McKinnon of Corry to Ranken re. sale of lands in Trotternish, 13 November, 1847; Barron, *Northern Highlands*, II, pp.329-330.

34. SRO, Loch Muniments, GD268/224, Lady Stafford to James Loch, 1 December 1832.

35. Thompson, 'Land Market', pp.268-308; Cannadine, 'Aristocratic Indebtedness', pp.628-9; Stone and Fautier Stone, *Open Elite*, pp.157-9.
36. Richards, *Highland Clearances,* II, p.417.
37. Cannadine, 'Aristocratic Indebtedness', pp.628-9; Thompson, *English Landed Society*, p.286; David and Eileen Spring, 'The Fall of the Grenvilles, 1844-8', *Huntington Library Quarterly*, XIX (1956); F.M.L. Thompson, 'The End of a Great Estate', *Economic History Review*, 2nd ser., VIII (1955).
38. James Hunter, *The Making of the Crofting Community* (Edinburgh, 1976).
39. SRO, Riddell Papers, GD1/395/26, Correspondence relative to a Disentail of Ardnamurchan by Sir James Riddell, November 1848.
40. SRO, Lord Macdonald Papers, GD221/62, General View of the Affairs of Rt. Hon. Lord Macdonald, 3 February 1846.
41. SRO, Clanranald Papers, GD201/7, Reports on Estate (1797); SRO, Brown MSS., TD80/100/4, Statement of Seaforth Affairs, 184-5.
42. Dunvegan Castle, Macleod of Macleod Muniments, 3/15831/1, Circular stating Macleod debts and assets, 7 April 1849.
43. A.M. Sinclair, *The Clann Gillean* (Charlottetown, 1899), p.440; Duke of Argyll (G.D. Campbell), *Autobiography and Memoirs* (London, 1906), I, pp.67-8, 129; Richards, *Highland Clearances*, II, p.418.
44. Shaw, *Northern and Western Islands of Scotland*, pp.43-6.
45. *Ibid*.
46. F.M.L. Thompson, 'English Great Estates in the Nineteenth Century (1790-1914)', in *Contributions to the first International Conference of Economic History* (Paris, 1960).
47. SRO, Lord Macdonald Papers, GD221/62, General View of the Affairs of Rt. Hon. Lord Macdonald (1846); Dunvegan Castle, Macleod of Macleod Muniments, 3/78-84, Abstract of Accounts, 1817-56; SRO, Riddell Papers, AF49/6, Report of T.G. Dickson for Ardnamurchan Trustees (1852).
48. SRO, Riddell Papers, GD1/395/26, Correspondence relative to a Disentail of Ardnamurchan by Sir James Riddell (1848).
49. See, generally, G.E. Mingay, *English Landed Society in the Eighteenth Century* (London, 1963).
50. Thompson, *English Landed Society*, pp.104-8.
51. Cannadine, 'Aristocratic Indebtedness', p.625.
52. F.M.L. Thompson, 'English Landownership: the Ailesbury Trust, 1832-56', *Economic History Review*, 2nd ser. XI (1958); Thompson, *English Landed Society*, pp.290-1; Spring, 'English Landed Estates', pp.16-19.
53. SRO, Lord Macdonald Popers, GD221/62, General View of the Affairs of Rt. Hon. Lord Macdonald (1846).
54. SRO, Brown MSS., TD80/100/4, State of Account, Earl of Seaforth, Rental etc. (1826).
55. Dunvegan Castle, Macleod of Macleod Muniments, 3/838, N. Macleod (?) to General Kyd, 6 February 1820.
56. *Ibid*., 4/1583/1, Circular stating Macleod's depts, 7 April 1849.
57. There are full accounts in Malcolm Gray, *The Highland Economy, 1750-1850* (Edinburgh, 1957), Chs. 3-5 and Richards, *Highland Clearances*, Part 5.
58. Gray, *Highland Economy*, p.149.
59. T.M. Devine, 'Social Stability and Agrarian Change in the Eastern Lowlands of Scotland, 1810-40', *Social History*, 3 (1978), pp.331-346.
60. *Ibid*.

61. Richards, *Highland Clearances*, p.515.
62. SRO, Brown MSS., TD80/100/4, Statement of Account, Seaforth Estate (1826). 63. What follows is based on an examination of the Clanranald, Lord Macdonald, Seaforth and Macleod estate papers for the 1820s and 1830s. Location and full citation of the material is provided in the notes above.
64. *PP, First and Second Reports from Select Committee on Emigration* (Scotland), VI (1841), pp.10-11, 46, 89, 198; Devine, *Great Highland Famine*, Ch. 4.
65. In 1839, arrears on the Coigach section of the Cromartie estate had reached £3036 or 169 per cent of annual rental [SRO, Cromartie Estate Papers, GD305/2/84-121]; on the Macdonald estates in Skye and North Uist arrears in 1832 were valued at £10,214, just marginally less than the annual book rental of £10,462 [SRO, Lord Macdonald Papers, GD221/62, State of Macdonald Affairs (1832)]; on the Earl of Seaforth's Urquhart estate, arrears rose from £5360 in 1816/17 to almost £8000 in 1836 [SRO, Seafield Muniments, GD248/1408, Urquhart Rentals, 1816-1856]; in the three western parishes of the Sutherland Estate of Assynt, Edderachillis and Durness arrears amounted in 1836 to 197 per cent, 170 per cent and 162 per cent respectively of annual rental [National Library of Scotland, Sutherland Estate Papers, Dep. 313/2283-2302].
66. Shaw, *Northern and Western Islands of Scotland*, p.46.
67. *Ibid*.
68. Cannadine, 'Aristocratic Indebtedness', pp.633-7; B.E. Supple, *The Royal Exchange Assurance: a History of British Insurance, 1720-1970* (Cambridge, 1970), pp.330-48; S.G. Checkland, *Scottish Banking: a History, 1695-1973* (London, 1975), pp.416-17.
69. SRO, Lord Macdonald Papers, GD221/62, General View of the Affairs of the Rt. Hon. Lord Macdonald (1846).
70. Insurance companies, banks and trust funds mobilised for 'secure' investments in landed property by family lawyers were most significant in this. At his bankruptcy in 1848, for example, Walter Frederick Campbell of Islay owed no less than £300,000 to the Scottish Widows Fund Society, £132,000 to the Royal Bank of Scotland and £100,000 to four trusts. See SRO, GD64/1/347, Campbell of Jura Papers, Report to the Creditors of the late W.F. Campbell of Islay.
71. Large land sales in almost all the cases surveyed in this essay were usually preceded by the appointment of trustees for the creditors to supervise estate management.
72. SRO, Highland Destitution Papers, HD7/47, William Skene to Sir Charles Trevelyan, 23 February 1848.
73. *Inverness Courier*, 15 July 1835.
74. *Ibid*., 28 October 1835.
75. *Ibid*., 6 March 1839.
76. *Ibid*., 13 November 1839; 28 October 1840.
77. *Ibid*., 28 October 1840.
78. See several references in the *Inverness Courier* for these years.
79. *Scotsman*, 11 August 1849.
80. SRO, Campbell of Jura Papers, GD64/1/347, Report to the Creditors of W.F. Campbell of Islay.
81. Thompson, 'Land Market', p.292.
82. Richards, *Highland Clearances*, II, p.472.
83. SRO, Campbell of Jura Papers, GD64/1/347, Report to the Creditors of W.F. Campbell of Islay.
84. Rubinstein, 'New Men of Wealth', pp.139-140.

85. Gaskell, *Morvern Transformed*, pp.37-46.

86. Barron, *Northern Highlands*, II, pp.XXX-XXXII.

87. Fullarton and Baird, *Remarks*, pp.36, 42.

88. Richards, *Highland Clearances*, II, p.487.

89. Fullarton and Baird, *Remarks*, pp.36, 42; *PP, McNeill Report* (1851), p.XV.

90. This discussion of John Gordon of Cluny is based on J.M. Bulloch, *The Gordons of Cluny* (privately printed, 1911); *Gentleman's Magazine*, II (1858), p.310; *The Times*, 23 July 1858; SRO, Lord Advocate's Papers, AD58/86, Conditions in Barra and South Uist, 1846-49.

91. Christopher Smout, 'Tours in the Scottish Highlands from the Eighteenth to the Twentieth Centuries', *Northern Scotland*, 5 (1983), pp.99-122.

92. *Illustrated London News*, 15 January 1853.

93. W.G. Stewart, *Lectures on the Mountains or the Highlands and Highlanders as they were and as they are* (London, 1860), 309-310.

94. *Inverness Courier*, 28 October 1835.

95. W. Orr, *Deer Forests, Landlords and Crofters* (Edinburgh, 1982), pp.168-180.

96. Quoted in *ibid.*, p.40.

97. C.L. Duckworth and G.E. Langmuir, *West Highland Steamers* (Prestcott, 1967 ed.).

98 T. Mulock, *The Western Highlands and Islands of Scotland Socially Considered* (Edinburgh, 1850), p.160.

99. *Inverness Courier*, 13 July 1836.

100. *Ibid.*

101. *Ibid.*, 28 October 1835.

102. *Ibid.*, 28 August 1833.

103. Gaskell, *Morvern Transformed*, pp.57-80.

104. Barron, *Northern Highlands*, III, p.78.

105. *Ibid.*, p.307.

106. Orr, *Deer Forests*, p.40.

107. Rubinstein, 'New Men of Wealth', pp.127-140; Stone and Fautier Stone, *Open Elite*, pp.211-228.

108. *Ibid.*

109. Bateman, *Great Landowners, passim.*

110. Rubinstein, 'New Men of Wealth', p.131.

111. This discussion of the Mathesons draws heavily on Burke, *Landed Gentry* and A. Mackenzie, *History of the Mathesons* (Inverness, 1882), pp.34-71; *PP, Napier Commission* (1884), p.124.

Appendix

Purchasers of Estates in the Western Highlands and Islands, 1800-1860

The list which follows does not attempt to provide an exhaustive or definitive guide to all those who bought estates in the western Highlands and islands in this period. The background of those who acquired some small properties, for example on the island of Mull after the sales by the Argyll estates in the 1820s, has proved difficult to trace. However, the wide variety of source materials which has been scrutinised to compile the Appendix means that details have probably been discovered on the majority of major purchasers. It is unlikely that additional information will substantially alter the pattern which emerges below from this large sample.

Where possible information from literary sources has been validated against Valuation Rolls (after 1851, E106 series in the Scottish Record Office), Particular Register of Sasines (Scottish Record Office) and J. Bateman, *The Great Landowners of Great Britain and Ireland* (London, 1882). The following estate papers have also been scrutinised: SRO, Breadalbane Muniments, GD112; Campbell of Barcaldine MSS., GD170; Campbell of Jura Papers, GD64; Clanranald Papers, GD201; Cromartie Estate papers, GD305; Loch Muniments; Lord Macdonald Papers, GD221; Maclaine of Lochbuie Papers, GD174; Riddell Papers, GD1 and AF49; Seafield Muniments, GD248; Seaforth Muniments, GD46; Brown MSS. (temporary deposit). National Library of Scotland, Sutherland Estate Papers, Dep.313. Inveraray Castle, Argyll Estate Papers. Achnacarry Castle, Cameron of Lochiel Papers. Conon House, Mackenzie of Gairloch MSS. Dunvegan Castle, Macleod of Macleod Muniments.

Lord Abinger. Purchased Inverlochy Castle estate (Lochaber) in 1840. Exposed for sale at £68,000; sold for £75,150. [*Inverness Courier*, 28 October, 1849.]

Lady Ashburton's Trustees. Purchased Arisaig from Ranald George Macdonald (Macdonald of Clanranald) in 1826 for £48,950. Lady Ashburton was a member of the Baring family of bankers and financiers. [J. Barron, *The Northern Highlands in the Nineteenth Centry* (Inverness, 1907), II, p.329.]

Lord Ashburton. Purchased Kinlochlincart estate for £37,000 in 1853 from Sir J.J.R. Mackenzie of Scatwell. [*Inverness Advertiser*, 15 November, 1853.]

James Baillie. Purchased estate of Glenelg in 1837 for £77,000 from Lord Glenelg. In 1835 acquired Glentrome in Badenoch for £7350, £2050 above the upset price. In 1838 purchased Glensheil from William Lillingstone for £24,500 and Letterfinlay in 1851 for £20,000. Baillie was a scion of the Baillies of Dochfour. Euan Baillie, his father, was a member of this family; he was born in Inverness and then became a successful West Indian merchant in Bristol. James was his third son, a Bristol merchant who also prospered in overseas trade and became M.P. for Tralee and Bristol. In 1846, he was described by government relief officers in the western Highlands as 'a person of wealth'. [Sir B. Burke, *A Genealogical and Heraldic History of the Landed Gentry of Great Britain and Ireland* (London, 1875), Vol. I, 'Baillie of Dochfour'; *Inverness Courier*, 21 June 1837; 15 July 1835; 22 May 1851; *Witness*, 21 May 1851; *Parliamentary Papers, Correspondence relating to Measures adopted for the Relief of Distress in Scotland*, LIII (1847), 132, Pole to Coffin, 19 October 1846.]

James Baird. Purchased Knoydart in 1855. A member of the Baird family of ironmasters and coalmasters, fourth son of Alexander Baird. Knoydart was the last remaining property of the Macdonells of Glengarry. Sold by Mrs. Macdonnel and estate trustees. [Burke, *Landed Gentry*, p.47; J.C. Lees, *A History of the County of Inverness* (Edinburgh, 1897), pp.200-2.]

J. Bankes. Purchased Gruinard estate (Gairloch parish, Wester Ross) and Letterewe estate (Lochbroom parish, Wester Ross). Letterewe exposed for sale in 1837 at £11,500. [*PP, Relief Correspondence*, (1847); Major Halliday to Sir E. Coffin, 3 February 1847; *Scotsman*, 14 June 1837.]

Col. Cameron. Purchased Kenchreggan for £8000 in 1827 from Macdonald of Clanranald. [Barron, *Northern Highlands*, II, pp.329-330.]

Col. Campbell of Possil. Purchased estate of Auchnacroich (parish of Torosay, Mull) in 1830. [*PP, Report to the Board of Supervision by Sir John McNeill*, XXVI (1851), Appendix A, p.27.]

Mr.? Cheyne. Purchased island of Lismore. He was an Edinburgh advocate with estates in Linlithgow and Fife. [*PP, Report of the Commissioners of Inquiry into the condition of the Crofters and Cottars in the Highlands and Islands (Napier Commission)*, XXXII-XXXVI (1884), 2327, Q.36884.]

Francis W. Clark. Purchased the island of Ulva in 1835 for £29,500. He was 'educated to habits of business and was long in practice as a writer in Stirling'. [*PP, McNeill Report*, (1851), Appendix A, Evidence of F.W. Clark, p.10.]

Earl Compton. Rt. Hon. Douglas Maclean, future Marquis of Northampton. Acquired estate of Torloisk in Mull. [*PP, McNeill Report*, (1851), Appendix A, pp.16-17.]

Lord Cranstoun. Acquired estate of Arisaig. Lived at Bagter Manor, Ashburton, Devon, [*PP, Relief Correspondence*, (1847), Rev. D. McCallum to Sir E.P. Coffin, 9 January 1847.]

Lord Dunmore. Purchased Harris in 1834 for £60,000 from Norman Macleod of Harris. He was a Lowland proprietor who owned lands near Falkirk. [SRO, Lord Advocate's Papers, AD58/84, Conditions on the Isle of Harris; *PP, Napier Commission*, (1884), 859, Q,.13353.]

Edward Ellice. Purchased Glenquoich for £32,000 in 1840 from Duke of Gordon. Added Glengarry in 1860 for which he paid £120,000, 'a splendid stretch of country from Loch Oich westward'. Ellice was descended from a family of Aberdeenshire lairds but was more immediately related to Alexander Ellice, an advocate at the Scottish bar and then an American merchant in London. Edward Ellice was originally a merchant in London; eventually became joint Secretary to the Treasury (1830-2) and Secretary at War (1833-4). [Barron, *Northern Highlands*, II, pp.329-330; Burke, *Landed Gentry*, p.392; Anon., *The State of the Highlands in 1854* (Inverness, 1855).]

James Forsyth. Purchased estate of Drimnin (Morvern) from Maclean of Boreray. He derived from landed gentry in Banffshire. [P. Gaskell, *Movern Transformed* (Cambridge, 1968), p.35.]

Col. John Gordon of Cluny. Purchased Barra from James Menzies in 1838. In 1838/9 acquired most of South Uist from Macdonald of Clanranald. Undertook further land purchases between 1839 and 1841 from Macdonald of Bornish, Macdonald of Boisdale and Macdonald of Barra. The total outlay (exclusive of purchase price of Barra) totalled £173,729. By 1841 he owned all of Barra, Benbecula and South Uist. Gordon came from Aberdeenshire legal and farming stock. His father was a Writer to the Signet and Clerk of Session under Henry Dundas. He owned estates near Edinburgh and Slains in Aberdeenshire. [J.M.
Bulloch, *The Gordons of Cluny* (privately printed, 1911), pp. 18, 34; *Gentleman's Magazine*, II (1858), p.310; *PP, Napier Commission* (1884), 771, Q.12058.]

Angus Gregorson. Purchased estate of Acharn (Morvern) in 1808 for £14,500. He was a prosperous tacksman on the Argyll estates in Mull and had earlier acquired the estate of Durran, Loch Awe in 1795. [Gaskell, *Morvern Transformed*, p.28.]

Sir Hugh Innes. Purchased Lochalsh from Mackenzie, Earl of Seaforth. [*PP, Napier Commision* (1884), 1932, Q.30058.]

Duke of Leeds. Purchased Applecross in 1854 for £135,000. [E. Richards, *A History of the Highland Clearances* (London, 1985), p.487.]

William Lillingston. Purchased estate of Lochalsh. In 1838 owned the entire parish. He was 'a man of business' from Ipswich but resident on his west Highland estate: 'He affords indeed a very singular and striking instance of an English gentleman, accustomed to all the blandishments of refined society, taking up his permanent residence in a poor and remote country'. [A. Fullarton and C.R. Baird, *Remarks on the Evils at Present Affecting the Highlands and islands of Scotland* (Glasgow, 1838), p.46.]

Col. McBarnet. Purchased estate of Torridon from Mackenzie, Earl of Seaforth in 1838. The property had been exposed to sale in 1837 at an upset price of £14,000. McBarnet was described in evidence to the Napier Commission as 'a West Indian or North American planter'. [*Scotsman*, 23 August 1837; *PP, Napier Commission* (1884), 1916, Q.29863.]

Major Alan Nicolson Macdonald. Purchased estate of Moidart from Macdonald of Clanranald in 1827 for £9,000 and Waternish (Skye) from

Charles Grant, M.P. in 1831 for £13,000. [*Inverness Courier*, 21 December 1831.]

A. Macdonald of Dalilea. Purchased estate of Lochans from Macdonald of Clanranald in 1813. [Barron, *Northern Highlands*, II, pp.329-330.]

Alexander Macdonald of Glenaladale. Purchased island of Shona from Macdonald of Clanranald in 1813 for £6.100. He belonged to the oldest cadet branch of the Clanranald family. [Burke, *Landed Gentry*, p.843; Barron, *Northern Highlands*, II, pp.329-330.]

Alexander McEwan. Purchased estate of Sunderland in Islay from the trustees of the late Walter Campbell for £28,000 in 1846. McEwan was a Glasgow merchant and grocer. [Margaret C. Storrie, *Biography of an Island* (Port Ellen, 1981), p.149; *PP, Relief Correspondence* (1847), Pole to Coffin, 6 October, 1846.]

Lachlan Mackinnon of Corry. Purchased Letterfearn estate in 1834 in parish of Glensheil from Mackenzie, Earl of Seaforth for £15,000. [*New Statistical Account of Scotland* (Edinburgh, 1835-45), XIV, 195.]

Alexander Maclean of Coll. Purchased Isle of Muck from Macdonald of Clanranald for £997 in 1813. [Barron, *Northern Highlands*, II, pp.329-330.]

Alexander McNeill. Acquired estate of Gigha. [Burke, *Landed Gentry*, p.864.]

Duncan McNeill. Acquired estates of Colonsay and Oronsay from his brother Alexander (above). Created Baron Colonsay. Purchased Canna from Macdonald of Clanranald in 1826. [Fullarton and Baird, *Remarks*, p.33; Burke, *Landed Gentry*, p.864.]

Dr. Hugh Macpherson. Purchased Eigg in 1826 for £14,500 from Macdonald of Clanranald. Macpherson was Professor of Greek in King's College, Aberdeen. [*New Statistical Account*, XIV, p.168.]

Sir Alexander Matheson, Bt.. Between 1840 and 1866 purchased the following properties in the western Highlands as well as buying estates to the value of £185,000 in Easter Ross: Ardintoul and Letterfearn (Lochalsh), £15,500 in 1840; Inverinate (north side of Loch Duich), £30,000 in 1844; Lochalsh, 'the ancestral possessions of his house',

£120,000 in 1851; Strathbran and New Kelso, £26,000 in 1866. His final possessions totalled 115,000 acres bought at a cost of £238,000. Matheson had made his fortune in the East India trade, firstly in the house of his uncle, James (Jardine, Matheson and Co. of London). About 1839 he returned to the Highlands 'with a magnificent fortune'. [A. Mackenzie, *History of the Mathesons* (Inverness, 1882), pp.41-45; Burke, *Landed Gentry*, II, p.902.]

Sir James Matheson. Purchased estates of Achany and Gruids in his native Sutherland in 1840 and the island of Lewis from the Mackenzie Earls of Seaforth in 1844. Made his fortune in opium trade and general commerce in Canton and Macao. [Mackenzie, *History of the Mathesons*, pp.60-64; *Inverness Courier*, 13 November 1839.]

James Menzies. Purchased Barra from McNeill of Barra in 1839. The upset price was £36,000 but he had to pay £42,050. Sold it shortly afterwards to Col. John Gordon of Cluny (see above) for £38,050. [*Scotsman*, 5 April 1837; Barron, *Northern Highlands*, II, pp.329-330; *Inverness Courier*, 6 March 1839.]

James Morrison. Purchased estate of Islay in 1852 for £451,000 after it had been exposed to sale in 1848 for £540,000. Morrison was a native of Hampshire but 'of Scotch extraction'. He was head of the mercantile firm of Morrison, Dillon and Co. of London and also owned large estates in Berkshire, Kent, Wiltshire and Buckinghamshire. He was M.P. for St. Ives (1830) and Ipswich (1832). One writer describes him as ' . . . possibly the richest British commoner of the nineteenth century'. [SRO, Campbell of Jura Papers, GD64/1/347, Report to the Creditors of the late Walter F. Campbell; Burke, *Landed Gentry*, II, p.952; W.D. Rubinstein, 'New Men of Wealth and the Purchase of Land in Nineteenth Century England', *Past and Present*, 92 (1981), p.131.]

David Nairne, Purchased estate of Aros (Mull) from Hugh Maclean of Coll in 1842 for £33,000. At this date Nairne also owned the estate of Drimkelbo. He sold Aros to Alexander Crawford in 1845. [*PP, Napier Commission* (1884), 2235, Q.35397.]

George Rainy. Purchased islands of Raasay and Rona in 1846. [*PP, McNeill Report* (1851), Appendix A, p.38.]

John Ramsay. Purchased estate of Kildalton in Islay in 1855 for £70,765. Ramsay was a merchant in Glasgow and whisky distiller. [*Inverness*

Marquis of Salisbury. Purchased the island of Rhum for £24,000 in 1845. [Barron, *Northern Highlands*, III, p.78.]

Patrick Sellar. Purchased estates of Acharn (Morvern) in 1838 for £11,250 and Adrtornish (Morvern) in 1844 for £11,100. Sellar was a lawyer and estate factor from Morayshire. [Gaskell, *Morvern Transformed*, pp.40-1.]

John Sinclair. Purchased estate of Lochaline (Morvern) in two sections in 1813 and 1821 for £17,500. Sinclair came from Highland tacksman stock and became a prosperous general merchant and distiller at Tobermory in Mull. [Gaskell, *Morvern Trnsformed*, p.30.]

Octavius Smith. Purchased estate of Achranich (Morvern) in 1845. Smith was a wealthy London distiller. [Gaskell, *Morvern Transformed*, pp.57-8.]

Christina Stewart. Purchased Glenmorvern (Morvern) in 1824. [Gaskell, *Morvern Transformed*, p.33.]

Duke of Sutherland. Purchased Reay estate in parishes of Tongue, Durness and Edderachillis in Sutherland for £300,000 in 1829. [Barron, *Northern Highlands*, II, pp.329-330.]

Lord Ward. Purchased Glengarry estate in 1840 from Duke of Gordon. It was sold to him 'after many offers' for £91,000, £3000 more than the upset price. [*Inverness Courier*, 28 October, 1840.]

Index